songwriting

songwriting

sam inglis

For over 60 years, more than 50 million people have learnt over 750 subjects the **teach yourself** way, with impressive results.

be where you want to be
with **teach yourself**

The publisher has used its best endeavours to ensure that the URLs for external websites referred to in this book are correct and active at the time of going to press. However, the publisher and the author have no responsibility for the websites and can make no guarantee that a site will remain live or that the content will remain relevant, decent, or appropriate.

For UK order enquiries: please contact Bookpoint Ltd, 130 Milton Park, Abingdon, Oxon OX14 4SB. Telephone: +44 (0) 1235 827720. Fax: +44 (0) 1235 400454. Lines are open 09.00–17.00, Monday to Saturday, with a 24-hour message answering service. Details about our titles and how to order are available at www.teachyourself.co.uk

Long renowned as the authoritative source for self-guided learning – with more than 50 million copies sold worldwide – the teach yourself series includes over 500 titles in the fields of languages, crafts, hobbies, business, computing and education.

British Library Cataloguing in Publication Data: a catalogue record for this title is available from the British Library.

First published 2007

This edition published 2007

The **teach yourself** name is a registered trade mark of Hodder Headline.

Typeset by Transet Limited, Coventry
Printed in Great Britain for Hodder Education, a division of Hodder Headline, An Hachette Livre UK Company, 338 Euston Road, London NW1 3BH, by Cox & Wyman Ltd, Reading, Berkshire.

Hodder Headline's policy is to use papers that are natural, renewable and recyclable products and made from wood grown in sustainable forests. The logging and manufacturing processes are expected to conform to the environmental regulations of the country of origin.

Impression number 10 9 8 7 6 5 4 3 2 1
Year 2012 2011 2010 2009 2008 2007

contents

01	**introduction**	**1**
02	**tools of the trade**	**4**
	guitar, keyboards or computers?	5
	why choose guitar?	6
	why choose keyboards?	7
	what guitar?	7
	acoustic guitars	14
	choosing a keyboard	18
	computers and songwriting	26
	other songwriting tools	36
03	**hooks**	**38**
	finding a vocal hook	42
	developing a hook	44
04	**basic theory**	**49**
	rhythm, melody and harmony	51
	bars and beats	52
	intervals, scales and chords	53
	chord sequences	62
05	**developing a hook**	**67**
	choosing a chord sequence	73
	developing a simple song from a chord sequence	76
	going back to our roots	77
	building from a hook	81

06	**developing lyrics**	**83**
	what are lyrics for?	84
	guided by voices	86
	voices and characters	88
	meter and rhyme	91
	rhyme schemes	96
	saying what we mean	97
	metaphor	99
	get into the details	101
	moving on	102
07	**song structure**	**103**
	how much variety do you need?	105
08	**arranging and recording your songs**	**109**
	what do I need to create an arrangement?	111
	more equipment for recording and arranging	113
	drum programming	118
	the basics of bass	123
	guitars	125
	keyboards	128
	other instruments	130
	arranging advice	131
	recording your vocals	132
	backing vocals and harmonies	138
	the finishing touches	140
09	**playing live and forming a band**	**143**
	where can I play?	144
	publicizing your gigs	149
	preparing for a gig	151
	on the night	153
	dealing with nerves	156
	if things go wrong	158
	after the gig	160
	starting a band	161

10	**promoting your music on the Internet**	**165**
	setting up a website	167
	setting up a MySpace music page	169
	other websites	175
	selling your music on the Internet	176
11	**the professional songwriter**	**178**
	publishing	180
	getting your songs in the public eye	182
	copyright	184
	writing for other people	185
index		**190**

01 introduction

In this chapter you will learn:

- **what this book can teach you.**

Can you teach songwriting? Lots of musicians would say that you can't.

It's true that writing a song isn't like mending your car, or cooking a meal. There's no recipe you can follow, no list of ingredients you can buy in Tesco. Many people believe that songwriting is about finding a way to express something personal that comes from deep inside you. Either you have the ability to do that, or you don't; and if you don't, there's no set of rules you can learn that will make it possible. In other words, it's all about natural talent.

You *do* have to have talent to write good songs, but the big mistake is to think that talent is something that only a few people will ever possess. We might not all have as much of it as the Paul McCartneys and John Lennons of this world, but all music fans have the talent to write songs, because the thing you need, above all else, is a passion and a love for music. And although the likes of Lennon and McCartney probably found it quicker and easier to learn the songwriter's skills than the rest of us, they weren't born with those skills. Everyone who wants to write songs has to teach him or herself how to do it.

Talent provides the spark, the individuality, the unique element that sets your songs apart from anyone else's. You can't teach yourself to have talent, but you can and must teach yourself how to harness the talent you already have.

Part of the reason why lots of people tend to think that songwriting can't be taught is that for them, the process of learning how to do it wasn't a conscious one. When we learn to play the guitar, someone else shows us where to put our fingers on the fretboard; many of us even have formal lessons. Songwriting, on the other hand, is something most of us end up figuring out for ourselves. Trial and error, constant practice and a lot of thoughtful listening to other people's songs all contribute to our education. What we end up with isn't a method that you could write down as a set of instructions, but a set of vague feelings that tells us when our ideas are working, and suggests avenues for developing them. Nevertheless, it's still something we have to learn how to do, and that means it's possible to teach yourself in a conscious as well as an unconscious way.

This book won't give you any foolproof recipes for writing songs, and it won't take away the need to practise. What it will do is give you a kind of toolkit that you can use to identify your best ideas and develop them into songs. The idea is that this toolkit should be accessible to anyone who has a passion for music: you don't need to be able to 'read' musical notation, or even play a musical instrument. Those skills are very valuable, and if you're lucky enough to have them, you'll have a much wider range of songwriting tools at your disposal, but the basic approach outlined here doesn't demand them.

Over the last two decades, technological change has had a radical effect on the way pop and rock music is created. Developments such as sampling, MIDI sequencing and loop-based recording have made us re-evaluate our very idea of what constitutes a song. They've changed the role of the professional songwriter out of all recognition, and more importantly, they've introduced hugely powerful songwriting tools that simply didn't exist in the 1960s or 1970s. If you know how to exploit these tools properly, you can write songs without being able to play a conventional instrument, and you can create finished recordings that sound slick and polished. One of the things that will make this book different from many songwriting guides is that digital music technology, and the new approaches to songwriting it makes possible, will be covered in detail alongside the more familiar guitars and pianos.

The music industry has changed along with technology, and the other main difference between this book and traditional songwriting guides is that the toolkit described here is tailored to modern ideas about what makes a hit song. We're used to thinking in terms of catchy tunes or memorable words, but the most important buzzword in the music industry is 'hooks'. A hummable melody or a distinctive lyric can be the basis of a hook, but there's a lot more to the idea than that. The approach to songwriting described here begins with understanding what makes a hook. We'll look at ways to come up with your own hooks, before thinking about how these can be developed into longer song sections and, ultimately, into complete songs.

Most people who write songs do so because they want to reach an audience, so the last section of this book will cover some of the ways you can bring your work to the wider world. One way is to get on stage and play live, and we'll be looking at the best ways to get gigs and build up an audience as a performer. Another way is to use the Internet, and this book will explain how to make your music stand out among the countless millions of MySpace wannabes. Finally, we'll look at how the music business relates to songwriters, and what you need to do if you want to turn your passion for songwriting into a career option.

tools of the trade

In this chapter you will learn:

- **whether you need to play a musical instrument to be a songwriter**
- **how to choose from the many types of guitar and keyboard that are available**
- **how computer software can provide an alternative to conventional instruments**
- **what you can buy to help you write down and remember ideas.**

You don't need to be a virtuoso musician or a great singer to be a good songwriter, but songwriters can usually play an instrument as well as sing. A song is more than just a tune and some words. Most songs are incomplete without some sort of musical backing, even if that's no more than a few strums on the guitar. If you want to play your songs in public, or have a band learn them, you'll need to do more than just sing the words. Guitar or piano chords are as much a part of the song as the title, and you need to be able to make the right choices and write them down.

There are two exceptions to this rule. The first is that, if you don't play an instrument, you can choose to collaborate with someone else who does. This is a good option for writers who specialize in lyrics; but, of course, it depends on you finding someone to be Burt Bacharach to your Hal David. Collaborative writing will be covered later on in this book, but for the most part, it will be assumed that you want to write songs on your own.

The second is that, thanks to modern technology, it's now possible to create a musical backing without touching a conventional instrument. Instead of playing guitar or piano yourself, you can use a computer to piece together fragments of music that other people have already recorded. Rap and hip-hop tracks have always been made this way, and it's an increasingly popular option for songwriters in other fields too. Traditional musicians often think of this approach as cheating but, in the right hands, it can be creative and very effective. It also requires a fast computer and some specialized hardware and software, and if you're attracted to this form of writing, there is advice on what to buy later in the chapter. Before that, though, let's consider the needs of songwriters who want to work in the more traditional vein.

Guitar, keyboards or computers?

Any musical instrument can be useful to the songwriter, but the vast majority of writers work with a guitar, or some sort of keyboard instrument like a piano. There are various reasons for this. Firstly, these instruments let you sing and play at the same time, which is not really an option with a saxophone or flute. Secondly, they can play more than one note at a time, which is a great help in nailing down one important component of a song: the chords, or harmony. And thirdly, they have a central place in the sound of pop music, unlike the violin or tuba. The few songwriters who don't use a guitar or keyboard tend to rely on related instruments, like the mandolin or bass guitar. Those options won't be considered in detail here, because the really important choice is between guitar and keyboards.

Many people reading this book will already be guitarists or keyboard players, and many more will be in the early stages of learning. But if you haven't yet made up your mind, or you're thinking of switching, how should you decide?

One obvious thing to think about is what style of music you want to play. Most people are drawn to music first as fans, and the chances are that you want to write songs that sound like the songs you listen to. So if you idolize the Arctic Monkeys, and you want to make music in that vein, you'll want to take up the guitar. By contrast, if you want to be the next Elton John, the piano is the instrument for you. In general, guitars are king in rock and metal, and also folk music, while keyboard instruments are on top in mainstream pop and jazz.

If you like music in lots of different styles, the choice might not be obvious; and let's not forget that it can be a good thing to take the road less travelled. For example, piano-led tracks like 'Trouble' and 'Bedshaped' have helped Coldplay and Keane stand out from the indie-pop scene, which is usually dominated by guitar bands. One thing is for sure, though: it's a choice that will have a huge influence on how you write songs.

Why choose guitar?

- It's the most widely used instrument in modern music.
- Most people find the guitar easier to learn than keyboard instruments.
- You can learn guitar without having to 'read' music.
- Guitars are generally cheaper and more portable than keyboard instruments.
- Guitarists have more freedom to put on a show when they're performing.
- Learning the guitar will put you in a good position to learn related instruments like the bass guitar.

Why choose keyboards?

- Keyboard instruments can produce a huge range of sounds, including good imitations of many other instruments.
- The ability to play keyboards is very useful if you want to make recordings that sound like a full band.
- Learning to play keyboards should give you a grasp of music theory.
- There are many more combinations of notes available on keyboard instruments than guitars.

What guitar?

Guitarists face a fundamental choice: electric or acoustic? Again, the decision will be influenced by the type of music you want to play. If you're into metal and hard rock, you'll obviously want to play electric guitar, and if folk ballads are your thing, you won't. But in between those extremes, there's a huge area where both types of guitar are widely used. In both cases, there's a vast range available, and you can spend anything from under £100 to several thousand. In the long run, most guitarists end up owning both, but what's the best option for someone starting out?

Electric guitars

In some ways, the electric guitar is the easier option of the two. Electric guitars usually have thinner strings which are set closer to the fingerboard, so they're easier for the beginner to get to grips with – and you can make an impressive racket on an electric guitar even if you can barely play it.

The key thing to bear in mind if you buy an electric guitar is that it won't be much use on its own. Electric guitars are designed to be plugged into an amplifier, and if anything, it's the amplifier (or 'amp') that makes the biggest difference to how they sound. You should look to spend at least as much on the amplifier as on the guitar itself; you'll get no benefit from buying a good guitar if you play it through a horrible amp.

The amplifier consists of an electrical circuit that boosts the tiny signal coming out of the guitar, and one or more loudspeakers that turn the signal into sound. In some pricey systems these two components come in separate boxes known as 'heads' and 'cabs' (short for speaker cabinet), but for most purposes, a 'combo' amp including both is more suitable. Again, there's a huge range

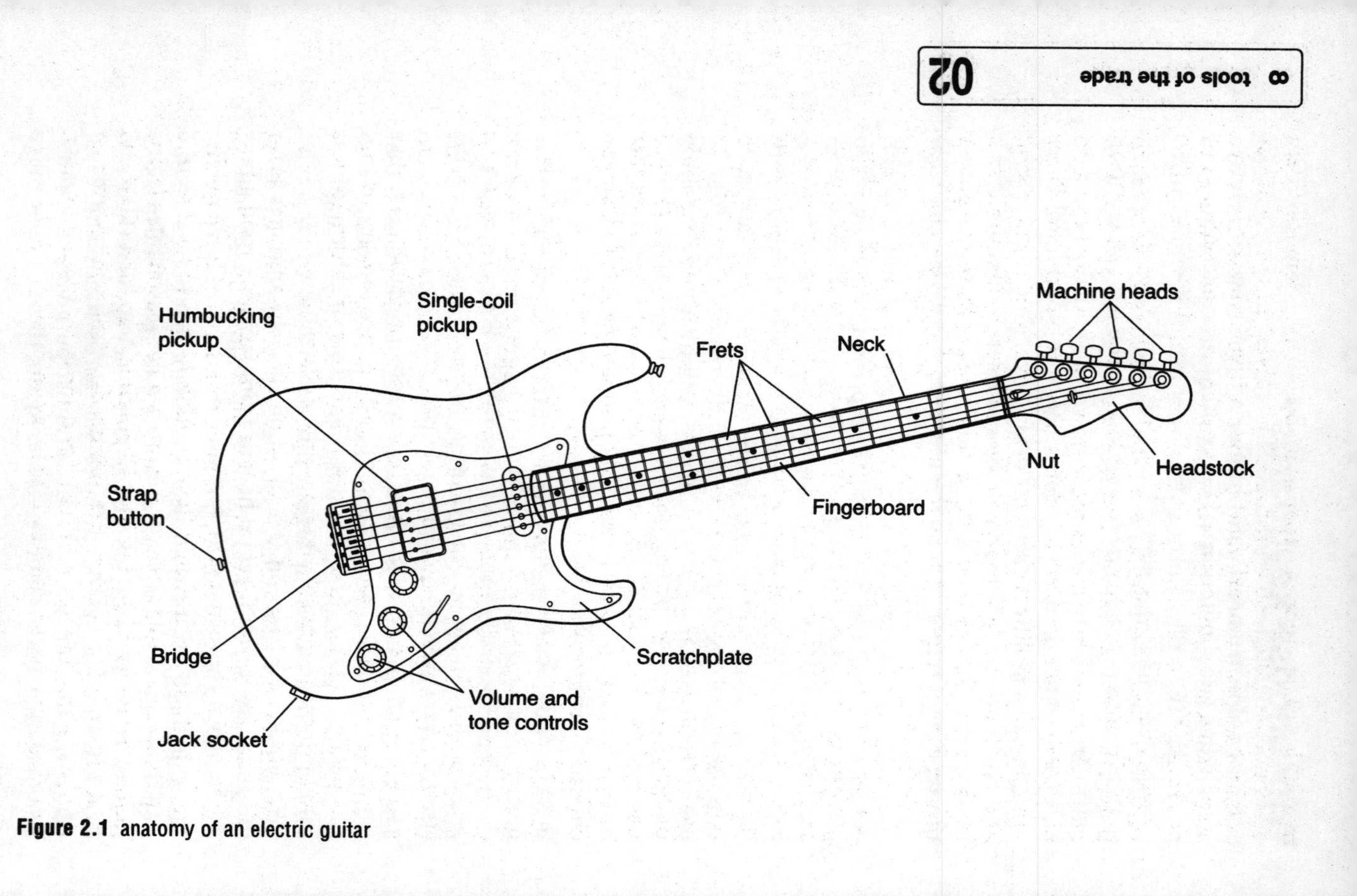

Figure 2.1 anatomy of an electric guitar

available. The more expensive ones use semi-obsolete components called vacuum tubes or 'valves' in the electrical circuit. Most guitarists think this gives a better sound, but valve amps also tend to be heavy, and the valves wear out and need to be replaced.

Like light bulbs, amplifiers are rated according to how much power they use up, from around five or six Watts up to 100W or more. An amplifier that uses more power will usually be able to play louder, but be aware that this is only a rule of thumb. There are 25 Watt amplifiers that will deafen everyone in the room, and 50 Watt models that will be completely inaudible if a drummer is playing at the same time. Apart from the power rating, other factors such as the number of speakers and their size also make a big difference.

When you buy your guitar and amp, it's crucial to think about how you'll be using them. The cheapest amplifiers tend to be small 10 or 15 Watt 'practice amps', which measure perhaps a foot (30 centimetres) square. These are intended only for use at home, and won't be loud enough to use with a band, even in rehearsals. Most of them also sound quite bad, and all in all, they are usually a false economy. Unless you're on a really tight budget, you will do better to get a bigger, louder amp, perhaps one rated at 30 to 50 Watts, with either a single 12-inch speaker or two 10-inch ones. Your guitar shop should be able to help you choose something suitable.

Another factor to bear in mind is that most amplifiers are designed to influence the sound of the guitar, either subtly or not so subtly. The gritty, aggressive guitars that you hear in rock and metal records sound that way because the amplifier is distorting the signal. Different amps do this in various ways, and can sound very different, so it's vital to try out a range of them. And if there's a guitarist whose sound you like, why not try to find out what amplifier he or she uses? This sort of information is often printed in guitar magazines and websites.

When it comes to the guitar itself, there are probably fewer ways to go wrong. Back in the 1970s, buying a cheap guitar made in the Far East was a minefield, but now, standards of build quality are so high that you would have to look long and hard to find anything truly unplayable. You can even get reasonable electric guitars for under £100, but if at all possible, aim for £150–£200 bracket or higher. There are hundreds, if not thousands of options within this price bracket, and most are made in China, or other Far Eastern countries such as Indonesia.

Figure 2.2 the Fender Stratocaster (left) and Gibson Les Paul (right) are the two most iconic designs of electric guitar

The two biggest names in electric guitars are Fender and Gibson. Their classic models such as the Fender Stratocaster and Gibson Les Paul are still costly, but both companies also make budget versions, under the names Squire and Epiphone respectively, which are very affordable.

Guitarists love to while away the hours discussing the tiniest details of their instrument, and how they affect the sound, but many of these differences are pretty hard for normal ears to make out. Electric guitars come in every conceivable shape and colour (and quite a lot that aren't readily conceivable) but underneath the skull logos and dragon scales, they're actually made of wood. Which wood is used for the body of the guitar does make a difference to how it sounds, but it's usually a subtle one. That's lucky, because specialist woods such as mahogany and rosewood carry a heavy price premium (and can contribute to the destruction of tropical rainforests). The shape has little effect on the sound of the guitar, but it can make a huge difference to how much you'll want to play it. Some novelty designs are impossible to play while sitting down, which is an obvious drawback. Others have awkward pointy bits that jab you in the ribs.

If you're new to the instrument, avoid buying a guitar with any kind of 'tremolo' system. The benefits that these bring – being able to make seagull noises and other novelty effects – are not worth the grief. Cheap tremolo systems invariably go out of tune, and make changing strings a pain.

Most electric guitars are made of solid wood, but you'll also come across so-called 'hollow bodied' designs. These tend to be more expensive than conventional electric guitars, because they are harder to make. They can be lovely guitars, and they do sound different from normal electric guitars, but don't buy one hoping to get something that sounds halfway between an electric and an acoustic. They might look a bit like acoustic guitars, but they are electric guitars at heart.

By far the most important factor in the sound of an electric guitar is its pickups. These are the components that turn the vibration of the strings into electrical current. Most guitars have two or three pickups, and their position on the body of the guitar makes a difference to how they sound. Typically, the pickup that's closest to the end of the strings (the bridge pickup) will be brighter and more cutting than the one closest to the fretboard (the neck pickup).

There are two main types of pickup, 'single-coil' and 'humbucking'. Classic Fender guitars such as the Stratocaster and Telecaster use single-coil pickups, which give a thinner, more twangy sound. Humbucker pickups are characteristic of Gibson guitars, and produce a sound that is rounder, fuller and often louder. Both types are used in all styles of music, though Fender-style guitars are more common in country music, while nearly all heavy metal guitarists use instruments with humbuckers. If you're in any doubt, you could always duck the issue and get a guitar with one of each.

Once you understand these basic facts, your best bet is to trust your instincts and your tastes. The right guitar for you might be someone else's idea of a complete nightmare, but the key point is that you need to choose something that makes you want to play it. With hundreds of instruments offering much the same features and build quality, it's not shallow to choose the one you think looks the best!

Get set up

Whether you buy an electric or an acoustic guitar, be sure to ask the shop to 'set it up' for you. This involves fine-tuning details such as the exact height of the strings above the fingerboard, and will make all the difference to how well the guitar plays. They should be willing to do this for nothing if they're selling you the guitar. If you buy a guitar off eBay or from the small ads in the paper, it's still worth taking it to a good guitar shop and paying 20 quid or so to have it professionally set up.

Effects pedals

If you're playing an electric guitar, you have the option of using foot pedals to generate special effects. These go between the guitar and the amplifier, and there's a truly vast range available. Some add very subtle movement to the sound, while others make the guitar completely unrecognisable. Some foot pedals just do one thing, while so-called 'multi-effects' offer a wide range of sounds. Effects can add variety and texture to the overall sound if you're playing with a band, and occasionally, the more radical ones can help you write songs you wouldn't have thought of otherwise.

Digital guitars

'Modelling' is a recent development which is beginning to have a profound effect on the world of the electric guitar. American company Line 6 invented two products, the Pod and the Variax, which use clever digital technology to make the electric guitar far more versatile. The Pod is like a miniature amplifier that can reproduce the sound of a whole range of other amplifiers, so you can imitate lots of classic guitar sounds without having to buy lots of amps. The Variax is a unique electric guitar that doesn't have conventional pickups. Instead, Line 6 have built in a system that 'models' other guitars, so in theory, the Variax can sound like a Fender Stratocaster, a Gibson Les Paul, and lots of other famous guitars. It even has a setting that sounds a bit like an acoustic guitar.

Line 6 and other companies such as IK Multimedia and Native Instruments have also applied the concept of the Pod to computer software. The idea behind products like the Line 6 Toneport, IK *Amplitube* and NI *Guitar Rig* is that you plug your electric guitar into your computer instead of a conventional amplifier. This gives you even more freedom to mess about with the sound, and is fantastic for recording, but it does have obvious drawbacks if you want to play with a band, or on stage.

Figure 2.3 line 6's Variax can imitate the sound of a wide range of other electric guitars

Acoustic guitars

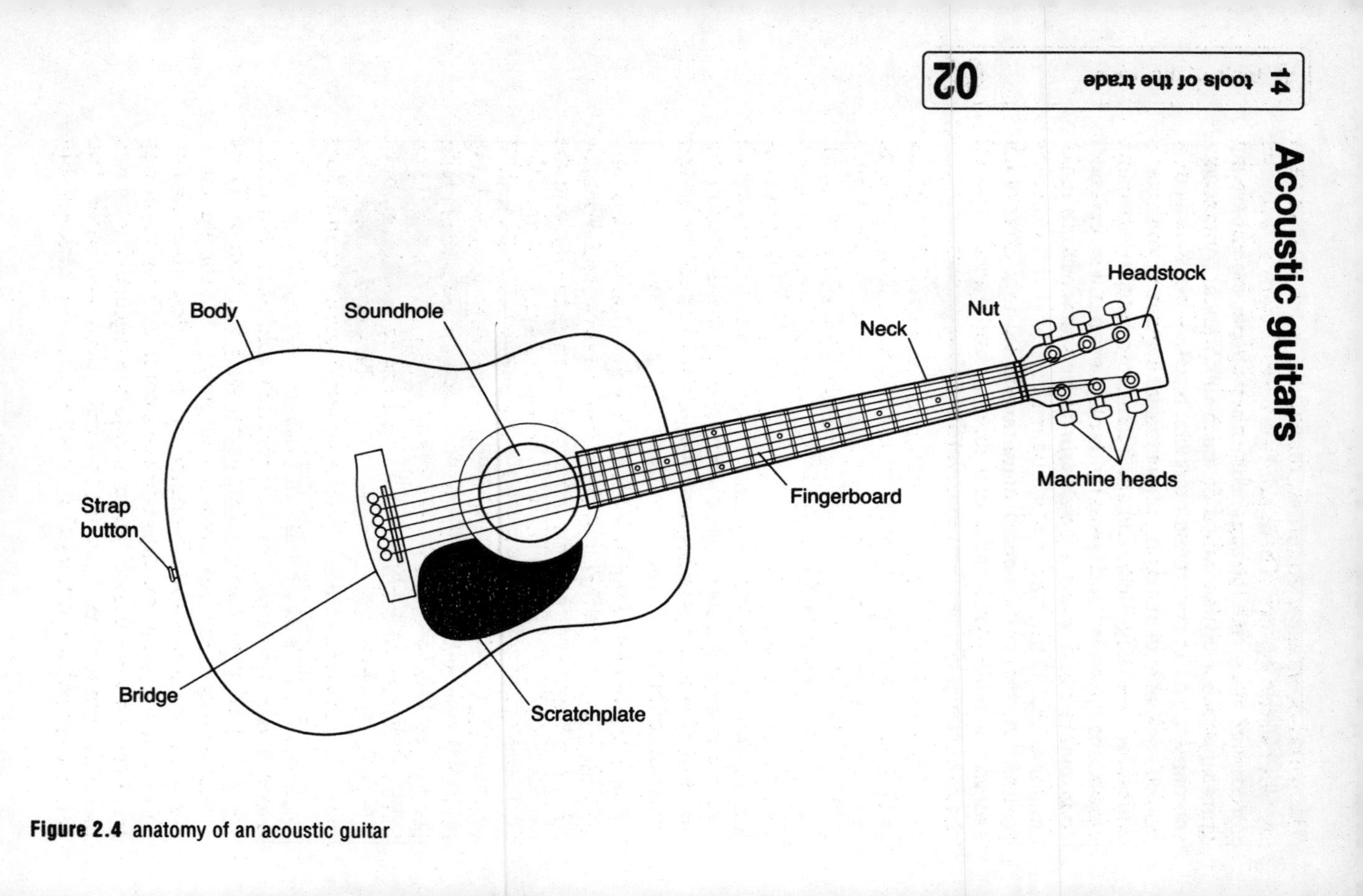

Figure 2.4 anatomy of an acoustic guitar

The world of acoustic guitars is, thankfully, much simpler than that of electric guitars. There are two basic designs of acoustic guitar: one uses steel strings, the other nylon. Nylon-strung guitars, which are also called Spanish or classical guitars, are sometimes used in pop music, but not often. When you hear a pop or rock musician talking about acoustic guitars, you can be confident that they mean the steel-strung variety. Steel-strung guitars are louder and usually larger than their classical counterparts, and make a brighter, zingier sound. Don't make the mistake of thinking you can turn one into the other by putting steel strings on a classical guitar: steel strings exert much greater tension on the instrument, and need special reinforcements which aren't built into classical guitars.

As with electric guitars, acoustic guitars are available at any price from under £100 to many thousands. By contrast, though, there's a relatively small range of shapes and sizes (see Figure 2.5). In general, larger instruments have a more full-bodied, booming sound, while smaller ones are brighter, thinner-sounding and quieter. The construction of an acoustic guitar is more complex than that of an electric guitar, and makes a much more obvious difference to the sound, so it's worth spending a bit more if you can – remember that you won't need to budget for an amplifier.

At the cheaper end of the market, the key question to ask of any acoustic guitar is whether it's made from pieces of solid wood, or from laminate. The cheapest guitars use only laminate, and the sound suffers as a result. The next level up have laminate sides and back, but use solid wood for the top or soundboard. If you're spending several hundred pounds, you'll get something that uses solid wood throughout. Unless you're on a really tight budget, it's always worth buying a guitar with a solid top. If you have the luxury of buying a guitar with solid wood top, back and sides, you may have options as to which wood is used. This makes much more difference with acoustic guitars than it does with electric ones, so try a few out.

If you're ever going to play live, whether solo or with a band, you will need to buy an acoustic guitar with a pickup in. These are sometimes called 'electro-acoustic' guitars, but should not be confused with the hollow-bodied electrics described earlier. Most acoustic guitar pickups work in a completely different way from the ones in electric guitars, and are normally mounted inside the guitar so that you can't see them from the outside. You can get special amplifiers that work with these pickups, but

Figure 2.5 acoustic guitars vary slightly in shape, and in the wood used to build them, but the basic design principles are usually constant

you're unlikely to need one: most music venues and rehearsal spaces will have a PA (public address) system, and the guitar should plug straight into that. At home, it'll be loud enough without amplification.

Often, the body shape and construction of 'electro-acoustic' guitars are optimised to make them sound good when plugged into a PA system. The down side of this is that they don't always sound as good unplugged. It is possible to add a pickup to an acoustic guitar that doesn't have one, but this is a job for a skilled professional – and even with skilled professionals, the results can vary.

Capos

One thing all acoustic guitar players should have is a capo. This is a device that fits across the neck and makes the whole instrument higher in pitch. Capos are widely used, and really extend the range of possibilities that is available to the guitarist. (They work with electric guitars too, though they aren't used so much.) If you're struggling to play along to a song on a record, or if you want to play a song but your voice can't hit the notes, experiment with a capo in different positions.

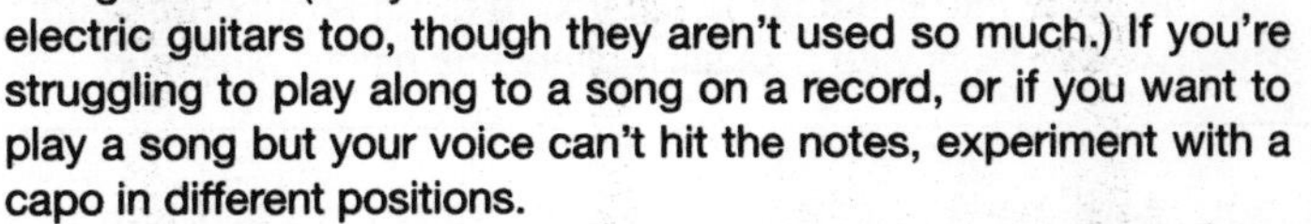

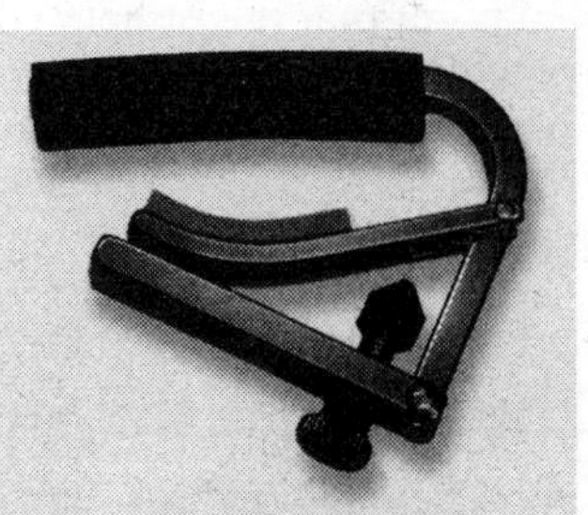

Figure 2.6 there are many designs of capo, but all have the same function: they fit across the fretboard of the guitar, raising the pitch of all the strings

Alternate tunings

The standard tuning for acoustic guitar is the same as for electric, but it's also quite common to use alternatives, especially in folk music. Nearly all of Nick Drake's songs, for instance, depend on the guitar being tuned in unconventional fashion. Experimentation with alternate tunings can be a fertile source of inspiration when you're writing songs, and also goes some way towards overcoming the restrictions of the guitar as an instrument. The nature of the guitar is such that it tends to 'push' you into using the chords that are easier to play, which can mean neglecting other possibilities. In alternate tunings, different chords become easy. A word of warning, though: if you use lots of alternate tunings, you have to be very careful when playing live to ensure that the audience doesn't end up sitting through five minutes of re-tuning between each song!

Perfect pitch

Electric and acoustic guitar players alike will probably want to invest in a guitar tuner. Most of these are designed to be used like the effect pedals described earlier: you plug the guitar into the tuner, and the tuner into the amplifier (if you're using an electric guitar). They will also work with acoustic guitars that have a pickup in.

If you're still wavering between electric and acoustic, there is one final point that might help you choose. For some reason, playing live with an electric guitar never, ever sounds good unless there's a band involved. Solo performers with electric guitars invariably become really grating, really quickly. So if you're likely to want to perform your songs on your own, get an acoustic guitar.

Choosing a keyboard

Keyboards, like guitars, can be electric or acoustic. Acoustic, in this case, means a piano, and there are two basic kinds: grand and upright. A Steinway or Bechstein grand would be on most keyboard players' list of 'Things To Buy When You Win The Lottery', but in the real world, few of us have the money or the space. An upright piano is a more realistic proposition, because they are smaller, cheaper and you can put them against a wall. But it's all relative: a new upright piano will cost several thousand pounds. You can pick them up much more cheaply second-hand, but you'll be lucky to get a good one for under £1,000, and there are plenty of pitfalls for the unwary. Unless it was a very good one in the first place, a piano will deteriorate over time to the point where it can no longer be tuned, and anything advertised as 'free to a good home' is likely to be unplayable and unfixable.

If you're lucky enough to have a good piano in the family house, by all means make that your songwriting tool. If you're choosing a keyboard for that purpose, though, you need to bear in mind the potential negatives. Pianos are not portable, so you can forget about taking one to a gig. They need regular tuning, which is expensive. And they don't have a volume control, so you may have to be careful if inspiration strikes at two in the morning. Finally, at the risk of pointing out the obvious, they only make one kind of sound – a piano sound. Most keyboard players will tell you that there is no real substitute, but at the same time, most will end up compromising by buying some sort of electronic keyboard.

There is a bewildering variety of keyboards out there, but most of them fall into one of a few fairly well-defined categories. Of these, some are more suitable than others for the would-be songwriter.

The actual keyboard is, of course, crucial. Most real pianos have 88 keys. Electronic keyboards are available in a range of sizes from 88 down to 25 keys. Larger keyboards make it possible to play a wider range of notes at once, but also make the keyboard more expensive and less portable. Most players would say that five octaves (61 keys) is the minimum acceptable compromise between the two.

Another term you'll hear is 'weighted action'. A weighted keyboard is designed to 'feel' like playing a real piano. As the name suggests, this means that the keys offer more resistance to the touch than in a non-weighted keyboard. If you learned to play on a real piano, you might find that non-weighted keyboards are quite hard to get used to, and many people feel that they are not as expressive. Weighted keyboards are, however, a lot more expensive to make and hence to buy, and also pretty heavy to lug about.

If you do go for a non-weighted design, make sure that it is 'velocity sensitive'. This means that the keyboard will respond to how hard you play each note, which is absolutely vital. And avoid buying any keyboard that has miniature keys; it'll be useless for learning and playing.

Electric pianos

Apart from actual pianos, all the keyboards you'll find in shops these days are electronic: if they're not plugged in, they won't do anything at all. However, there used to be pianos that worked along the same lines as an electric guitar. The keys actually made a faint tinkly sound using a mechanical action involving hammers and 'tines', but this was very quiet, so you needed to plug them into an amplifier to hear them. As with the electric guitar, you could shape the sound by changing amplifier settings or using effect pedals, but there was only one basic sound. Until recently, no-one had made a piano of this type for the best part of 20 years, but they are worth knowing about because the old ones are still used a lot in pop music.

There were three important designs. The Rhodes piano, often known as a Fender Rhodes, was the most common, and you can hear its distinctive bell-like sound on millions of records even today. In fact, it remains so popular that manufacture of a new model started in 2007 after more than 20 years out of production. The Wurlitzer EP200 worked along similar lines, and is also still hugely popular; it has a more rounded, chunky tone. Finally, there was the Yamaha CP70, a strange sort of electrified miniature grand piano which has recently been revived by Tom Chaplin from the band Keane. All three were victims of fashion in the 1980s, and as a result, there are still Rhodes and Wurlitzer pianos sitting in lofts and garages around the country, so it's sometimes possible to get lucky and pick one up for next to nothing. If you can, and you have the space, do. If not, don't pay the ludicrous second-hand prices that are often asked on eBay and the like. Almost all modern electronic keyboards can do a decent imitation of the electric piano sound, and are more convenient.

Stage pianos

Some electronic keyboards are designed to be direct substitutes for an acoustic piano. These come in two types: 'stage pianos', which are supposed to be relatively portable, and electronic pianos for home use, which are meant to be nice pieces of furniture. If you plan to play anywhere outside your living room, you'll want the former.

Stage pianos are invariably weighted and at least five octaves wide. They usually give you the option to make them sound like a Hammond organ, an electric piano or perhaps a double bass,

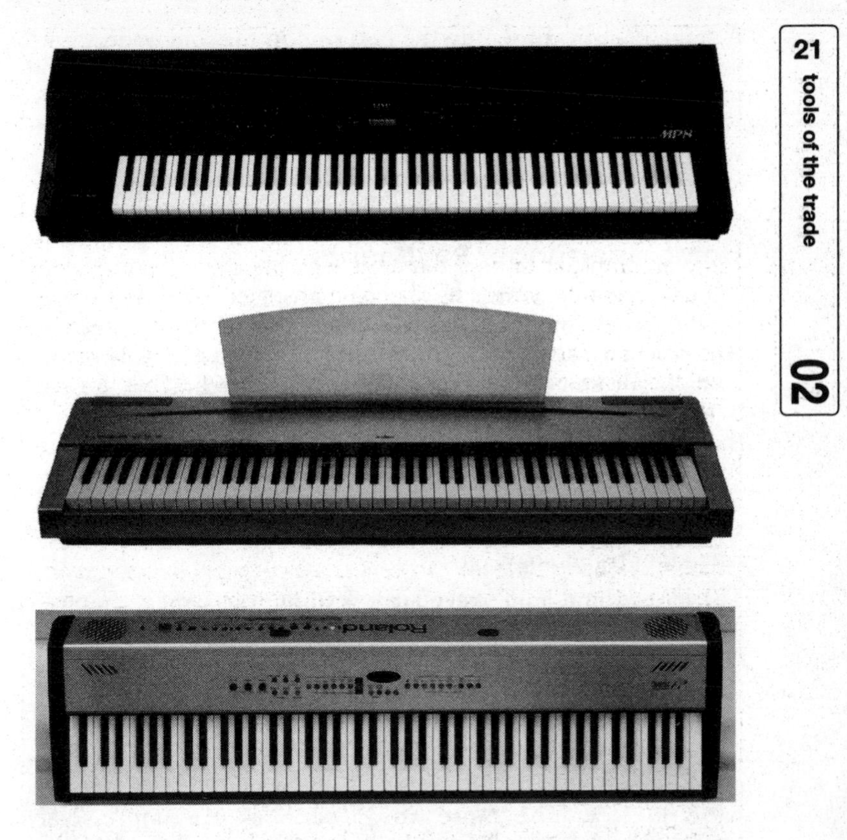

Figure 2.7 Kawai's MP series (top) is the Rolls Royce of stage pianos, but other manufacturers such as Yamaha and Roland also make popular models

but the main point is to mimic an acoustic piano, and the basic piano sound should bear a pretty good resemblance to the real thing. However, not all stage pianos include loudspeakers to let you hear it. If not, you'll need to plug yours into a pair of headphones, an amplifier, or a hi-fi to hear it. Keyboards with loudspeakers are convenient for playing at home, but the built-in speakers won't be loud enough to let you play with a band or on stage. Most rehearsal rooms and all music venues will have a PA system that you can plug your stage piano into to amplify it.

The best stage pianos are those made by Kawai, though their MP series is not cheap. Other major manufacturers include Yamaha, Korg and Roland. You can expect to pay at least £500 for a new stage piano.

A stage piano is probably the best option for songwriters who want to work in the classic vein of artists like Elton John, and if you're a good piano player it will enable you to use that skill to best advantage. If, on the other hand, you want to experiment with a variety of sounds, or create fuller-sounding backing tracks for your songs, stage pianos probably aren't for you.

Home or arranger keyboards

These days, lots of music is faked. From drum kits and bass guitars to any orchestral instrument you can think of, the fact that you can hear it on a record no longer means it was played by a real drummer, bass player or violinist. Technology has got to the stage where even those in the know can find it hard to tell the real thing from the imitation. But that doesn't mean it's easy to manufacture a convincing rhythm section or string quartet. The faked arrangements you hear on records and TV soundtracks are created by people who have a lot of expertise in using that technology.

The idea behind home keyboards is to put the same technology into a form that doesn't require any expertise. What this means in practice is that all the hard work is done by the designers of the instrument, rather than the player.

This sort of instrument will usually present you with a choice of 'styles', with names like Swing or Pop Ballad; you choose the one that best suits your song, and off you go, instant backing band in tow. The more advanced ones are impressively sophisticated, with realistic sounds and the ability to follow your playing and make sensible musical choices. Their major selling point is their ability to mimic backing musicians that can play along with you, but home or 'arranger' keyboards can be played like a piano or organ, and the most expensive ones have good weighted keyboards. They have a much wider range of sounds than most stage pianos, they invariably have built-in loudspeakers, and should have the ability to connect to a PA system if needed.

However, a home or arranger keyboard is probably not a good choice if you have a serious interest in songwriting. There are two main reasons for this. The less serious one is that within professional music circles, home keyboards are universally seen as naff. This perception is a little unfair, because it's partly a hangover from the days when 'home keyboard' meant a cheesy organ with one of those boom-tish drum machines attached. Nevertheless, the only professional musicians you'll see playing this type of instrument are the ones doing winter season on cruise ships, singing Abba medleys.

The main reason is that home keyboards tend to stifle creative freedom. They're mainly intended for performers who want to play other people's songs, and there's a flourishing cottage industry that turns the latest pop hits into arrangements you can load into your home keyboard. You don't have to do that, it's true, but even so, you'll be working with a limited range of musical patterns. Unless you turn the arranger section off and use it like a stage piano, chances are you'll feel as though the cart is pushing the horse. As we'll see, the ability to produce decent quality backing tracks for your songs is useful, and vital if you want to be a professional songwriter; but they need to be your backing tracks, not some generic idea of a pop ballad cooked up by a keyboard designer in Japan.

Workstation synthesizers

There are many similarities between this next class of instrument and the home keyboards we just dismissed. Like home keyboards, workstation synthesizers are designed to produce a wide range of sounds, and many of these sounds are substitutes for real instruments. Like home keyboards, they are capable of playing back lots of these sounds at the same time to create the illusion of a real band backing you up.

The key difference is that workstation keyboards don't force you into working with someone else's idea of a musical style (though some of them do include this sort of technology as well). It's completely up to you to choose different sounds, and to tell them what to play. If you want to, you can get deeply into 'programming' every little detail of a backing track. You also have lots of freedom to change the sounds and add effects to them. And, of course, you can use them like a stage piano if you want to. Bear in mind, though, that these instruments almost never include loudspeakers, so you'll need to connect headphones or a hi-fi to hear anything.

Workstation synthesizers are usually available in two or three different keyboard sizes, with the option of weighted keys for those who want them. You can expect to pay anything from £400 up to well over £1,000, depending on what features you want. Top of the heap by a small margin is Korg's Triton range, which are the ones you're most likely to see in the hands of professional musicians, but there's also a lot to recommend rivals like Yamaha's Motif series and Roland's Fantom X. More

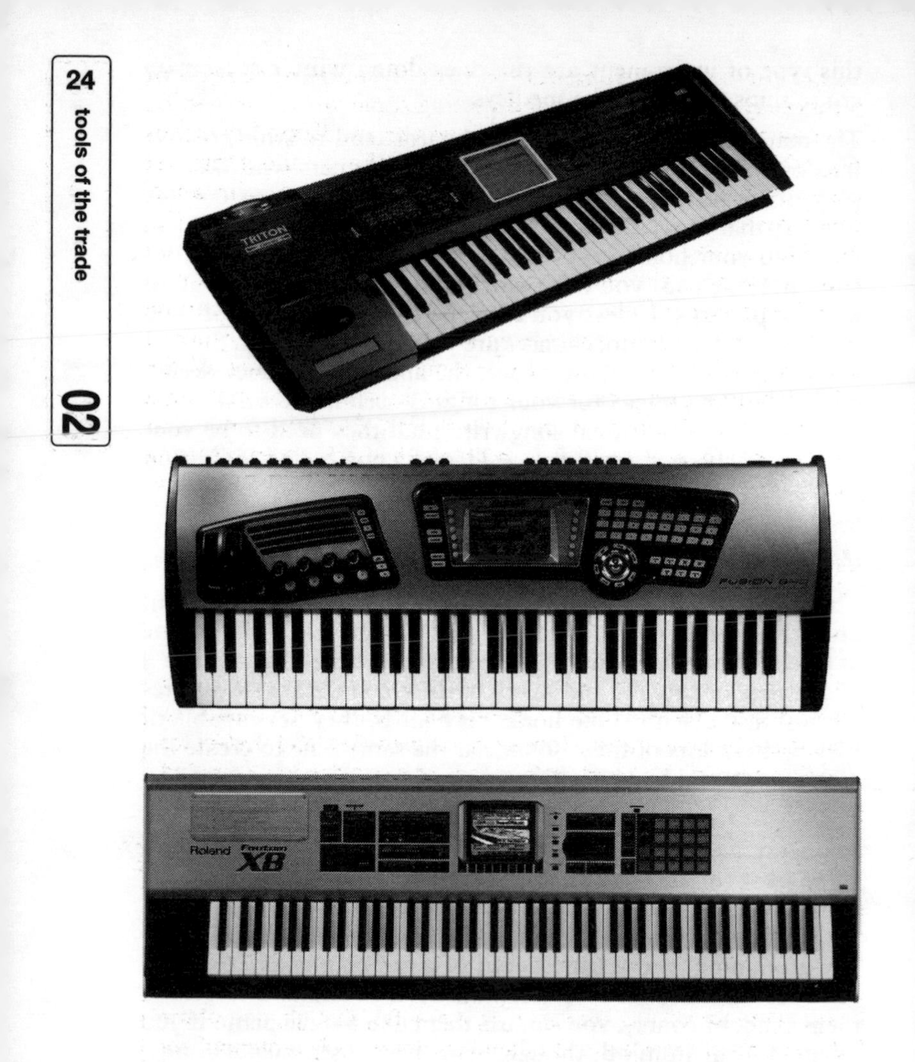

Figure 2.8 Korg's Triton Extreme range (top) arguably leads the workstation synthesizer market, but other models such as the Alesis Fusion (centre) and Roland Fantom X (bottom) have much to recommend them

affordable alternatives include Roland's new Juno-G and Alesis's Fusion. You could also investigate second-hand options: an older professional model such as a Korg Trinity, Kurzweil K2000 or Yamaha EX7 is an attractive alternative to a newer budget keyboard.

So are these the instruments for you? If you're not afraid of technology and you don't mind putting some work into getting to know your instrument, yes. Their power and flexibility means that it's possible to create backing tracks that sound great, yet are individual enough to stand out from the crowd. For instance, songwriter Rob Davis created the Kylie Minogue hit 'Can't Get You Out Of My Head' almost entirely on his Korg Triton. And at the same time, they make excellent tools for live performance. The down side, of course, is that workstation synths can be pretty complex. Quite apart from learning to play the keyboard itself, it'll take you a while to become skilled at using all the other features, and creating a good backing track or making a cool new sound can be a lot of work. It's also fair to say that most people making records now create the backing tracks using computer-based tools, and it's less common to use a workstation keyboard alone for this.

Other keyboards

It's worth mentioning a few other types of keyboard in passing. Firstly, there are synthesizers that concentrate solely on the 'making cool sounds' aspect of keyboard playing, and aren't intended to produce realistic imitations of other instruments, or complete backing tracks. These can be great fun, and perfect for adding interest to a band performance or a backing track created elsewhere, but they are usually too limited to be much use for songwriting (some don't even have keys!). Pre-digital synthesizers from the 1970s and early 1980s fall into this category, and are highly prized on the second-hand market.

Secondly, there's another instrument with numerous electric and acoustic variants: the organ. Like the Rhodes piano, the vintage Hammond B3 is a staple sound in pop and rock music. You're unlikely to be able to afford, or lift, a real B3, though, and of the thousands of other electric organs out there, only a handful are still highly regarded. In the right hands, the organ can be an instrument that offers unique creative possibilities, but it's not an ideal first keyboard for a would-be songwriter. Any stage piano or workstation synthesizer will do a passable B3 imitation, but there's no way to make an organ sound like a piano.

Finally, there are so-called 'controller keyboards'. Strange as it may seem, controller keyboards don't make any sound in their own right. Instead, as the name suggests, they're designed to trigger sounds in other devices, using a system called MIDI

(Musical Instrument Digital Interface). Controller keyboards are big news these days, and for good reason. More and more music production is being handled by computers, and there are computer programmes available that will easily surpass what is possible on even the most sophisticated workstation synthesizer. You can, if you want, 'play' your computer just as if it were a piano or any other instrument, and use it to record the results. But, of course, computers don't have keyboards, or at least not the sort with black notes and white notes. Controller keyboards are available in every shape and size, from miniature ones that will fit in a laptop bag, to battleship-sized 88-note monsters festooned with knobs and sliders.

Computers and songwriting

We're accustomed to thinking of writing songs and making records as two different activities, because that's how it used to be. Tunes and words would be thrashed out over a guitar and a strong cup of coffee, before musicians learned and developed the song. They'd rehearse it until they knew it backwards and play it to audiences up and down the country, before finally going into a recording studio to perform it for posterity. And the job of capturing that performance would belong to a technician, an engineer with no connection to the band, who might be recording Mozart symphonies the next day and Bulgarian folk music the day after that.

That was the way it worked because, at the time, that was the only way it could work. Recording equipment was colossally expensive and required rocket scientists to operate and maintain it. The idea that a musician could own, or even understand, the means of making a record would have seemed laughable.

Fast forward 30 or 40 years, and we find ourselves in a situation where nearly everyone owns the means of making a record. The PC you use for surfing the Internet and playing *Grand Theft Auto* is no different from the PCs that are used every day in recording studios across the planet. These machines are at the heart of the vast majority of the hit records you hear today. Not only have computers all but replaced recording devices like tape recorders; many of the sounds you're hearing on records were actually made by computer programmes.

At this point, you may be thinking: it's great that I have a virtual Abbey Road in my living room, but what does this have to do with songwriting? The answer is that as recording has become accessible to everyone, so the divide between writing songs and making records has all but disappeared. One of the most fundamental lessons that songwriters, and the music industry in general, have learned over the last 20 years or so is that great music is just music that sounds great. The traditional approach to songwriting is one way to make music that sounds great, but if you think about it, there are lots of ways it can go wrong. You're only going to end up with a great record if you write a brilliant song, find brilliant musicians to play it, and find the right engineer to record it. Lots of great songs have never been hits because they weren't played right, and lots of great musicians have wasted their talent on poor material. And at the same time, people who have never picked up a guitar in their lives have made great records by paying attention to how things sound. The Prodigy's 'Firestarter' is now thought of as a classic song, but Liam Howlett never sat down and picked out the chords on an acoustic guitar.

In other words, for many people, songs are important, but they're not the finished product. The finished product is what matters, and so the best way to approach music is to head straight for that. If can do that successfully, chances are you'll be writing a great song in the process.

One of the things that will make this book different from most songwriting manuals is that this approach will be taken seriously, and the ideas that will be presented should make it possible to write songs even if you don't play an instrument, or think of yourself as a musician. That is one of the biggest positives about the computer-based approach, and there are others, too. It gives you a kind of creative freedom that guitarists and pianists don't have; when it comes to putting together sounds, they are limited to the sounds those instruments can create. You're not. Moreover, learning to use computer-based music tools puts you at a huge advantage if you want to make records, or write songs professionally. These days, you can't hope to impress anyone with a demo recording of yourself singing and playing guitar. If you want to sell your song to someone else, chances are you'll be selling them a record with a hole where their voice should go.

So what are the down sides? The first is that there's a steep learning curve. You might not have to learn an instrument, in the traditional sense, but you will have to become familiar with the ins and outs of some pretty complex computer software. You'll also need to understand some of the principles of digital audio, which can be confusing to the uninitiated. Secondly, it's likely to get expensive. You can start with a cheap home PC and some free software downloaded off the Internet, but if you get into it, you'll find yourself wanting more and more additional equipment and a faster and faster computer. And thirdly, you won't have the same options when it comes to playing live, or collaborating with other songwriters.

The best of both worlds

Songwriters who start out with software usually end up learning to play a conventional instrument too, at least to some degree. In the end, most people find the best way to get guitars or pianos onto your recordings is to play them; and even if you never become Alfred Brendel, you'll find that knowing your way around a keyboard saves enormous frustration when you're working with computers.

What computer should I buy?

Many people will already have a recent PC at home, and this is likely to be a good starting point for trying out computer music-making, though as we'll see, you'll probably need to invest in some additional hardware. If you don't already have a PC, or your current model is a creaking Windows 95 job that is barely capable of surfing the Internet, what should you look for in a new model?

The power of computers develops so fast that the £400 model you buy from PC World today will, in performance terms, trounce the £2,000 specialist machine from a couple of years ago. You can definitely get a lot done even on such an entry-level machine, but it's likely to turn out to be a false economy if you get serious about computer music. Let's look at the most important features in a music computer.

Perhaps the most basic question is: 'Should I get a Windows PC or an Apple Mac?' Macs have only a tiny share of the general PC market, but they have traditionally been favoured by the creative industries, and you're far more likely to see Macs than PCs in professional music environments such as recording studios. There's quite a lot of music software that is only available for Macs, and in fact new Macs come with a programme called *Garage Band* that has a lot to recommend it for those starting out in computer music. Macs have a reputation for being easier to set up and use with music hardware than PCs, and there is probably still some truth in that, although Windows XP made huge strides in this department. The Apple operating system, Mac OS X, is pretty much invulnerable to the viruses and worms that plague PC users. Mac OS X is a mature and established platform, but Windows users face a potentially disruptive switch from XP to Vista in the near future, and questions remain about whether the 'digital rights management' features of Microsoft's new operating system will have bad consequences for music software. And now that Apple have switched over to using Intel processors in their machines, it's possible to install Windows on them and use them exactly like conventional PCs if you wish.

The down side of all this is that, pound for pound, Macs are more expensive than generic PCs offering the same basic level of performance. There's also a relatively limited range of hardware options such as graphics cards and hard disk drives. Many people like to build their own PCs from parts, which isn't possible with Macs. And if you want to use your computer for other purposes such as playing games or running office software, you'll find that Macs are less well supplied in these areas.

Another basic question is: 'Should I get a laptop or a desktop machine?' Here the answer is no different from what it would be when buying a computer for any other purposes. You'll know whether you need a laptop or not; if so, get one, if not, don't. Rest assured that it's perfectly possible to use all the necessary software and hardware on a laptop, but as ever, the same amount of money will buy you less in terms of raw performance, screen size and potential for expansion, all of which are important in this field. There are an increasing number of musicians using laptop computers as live performance tools; this is something to bear in mind, but be aware that bringing any sort of computer on stage can be a minefield for the unwary.

Whether you choose Mac or PC, desktop or laptop, the other factors you need to consider are pretty much constant. The first of these is the computer's central processing unit, or CPU. In Windows PCs you have a choice between models made by Intel and AMD, while all new Macs use Intel CPUs. If you're buying a Windows machine, you're also likely to have to choose between 32- and 64-bit CPUs, and between single- and dual-core designs. There's not space to get into the details here, and not much point, since the landscape changes so fast, but at the time of writing, relatively little music software is capable of taking advantage of 64-bit processing, and most music hardware is not supported under the 64-bit version of Windows.

This will change, and you can run 32-bit Windows and 32-bit music software on a 64-bit machine, but at the moment there's no reason to choose 64-bit unless you need it for other software that you want to run.

By contrast, it's definitely worth choosing a multi-core CPU. These designs, in effect, build two or even four conventional CPUs onto a single chip, allowing the workload to be divided as long as the software is written in such a way that it can exploit this feature. Nearly all the major music programmes are now multi-core compatible, and most of them offer huge gains in performance on multi-core systems.

One other thing to consider when choosing a CPU for a Windows machine is that both AMD and Intel offer budget versions of their main range, such as the 'Sempron' and 'Celeron' designs. If at all possible, these should be avoided, as they tend to save money by cutting back on the very features that help music software run fast.

Probably the second most important factor in terms of computer performance with music software is RAM. Basically, you'll need a lot of it: one gigabyte (1GB) is a sensible minimum. You'll also need a decent amount of storage space, as sound files take up a lot of room. This means a large hard drive, or better still, two hard drives: one for programmes, and one for sounds. If possible, make sure that the hard drives you get have a spin speed of 7,200 rpm or faster. This information isn't always easy to find out when you're buying a computer, but it will make a difference with music software. It shouldn't be a problem to find desktop machines with 7,200 rpm drives, but many laptops are still stuck with 5,400 rpm models.

By contrast, you don't need a fancy graphics card for music software, and in many ways it's better to get a fairly cheap one. Just make sure, if you're buying a desktop machine, that the graphics card is an AGP rather than a PCI model; and if you're getting a laptop, be sure to get one that has dedicated graphics hardware rather than 'shared graphics'. Although music software doesn't require cutting-edge graphics cards, it does benefit from being run on a large screen, or even more than one screen, so don't skimp here.

Noise pollution

One factor that's particularly important with computers for music is the amount of noise they make. Unless you have a really bad example, you probably aren't too bothered about the buzzes and whirrs that come from your home or work PC, but a noisy computer is a complete nightmare for music-making. It's especially important when buying a laptop to insist on hearing how loud it is when the cooling fans come on, which may mean leaving it switched on for ten minutes or so. Most laptops are fairly quiet until they get hot, but you want one that will be quiet all the time. Quietness is also important for desktop computers, though at least here you have the option of replacing fans and adding insulating foam if it gets too much.

Listening to computers

As if the business of choosing a computer weren't complicated enough, there are a few other things you'll need to choose too. The most obvious of these is some means of listening to your musical creations. Nearly all computers come with built-in loudspeakers, but these are always completely inadequate for the job. You need to be able to hear cleanly, at a decent level of loudness and without distortion to make the right decisions when you're putting a song together, and your computer's built-in speakers will absolutely not let you do that. Nor, to tell the truth, will those £29.99 desktop speakers you can get from PC World.

If you have a decent hi-fi, in other words one put together from 'separates' and with a good pair of speakers, you could do worse than plug the output from your PC into that. This has the huge advantage that you'll be listening to the music that you're making in exactly the same way as you listen to any other music, so you can make really informed judgements about how it compares. Make sure that the hi-fi is set up correctly, though, with the speakers properly positioned as described in the manual. Even an expensive system will be useless if the speakers are shoved behind the sofa or stuck on shelves.

If you don't have a good hi-fi, or you don't want to put your PC in the same room as it, the cheapest way to get reasonable sound quality is to invest in a good pair of headphones. In fact, sooner or later you'll want to get a good pair of headphones anyway. They have lots of advantages. For one thing, they let you hear in more detail than almost any pair of speakers. For another, you can listen to music on headphones at any time of the day or night, without risking a call from Environmental Health. And furthermore, headphones are essential if you want to record anything through a microphone, a topic that will be discussed further in Chapter 08. Bear in mind here that these positives only apply to good headphones: you should be looking to spend well over £50 on a pair. Cheap phones will be just as useless as cheap speakers.

Headphones do have their disadvantages, though, especially if you don't have loudspeakers as well. The main one is that listening to music on headphones is just so different from listening on speakers. The experience of getting really excited about something you're working on, burning it to a CD, playing it on your hi-fi and realizing that it actually sounds dreadful is one that you don't forget in a hurry, especially if you've got friends round at the time!

If you're buying a pair of loudspeakers just to use with the computer, you have a few options. Ordinary hi-fi loudspeakers will work, but you'll also need an amplifier to use with them, and somewhere to put them, which isn't always easy to arrange. If you can, you'll find something workable for £150 or so in a shop such as Richer Sounds, or less in the local pawn shop.

You can also buy good-quality versions of those cheapo desktop speakers, though naturally these are no longer quite so cheap: expect to pay upwards of £100 for typical models from Edirol and M-Audio, and many times that for serious professional systems like Blue Sky's Mediadesk. These are either powered from the computer or direct from the mains, so you won't need a separate amplifier, and they should be small enough to fit on even the dinkiest desk. Their main problem is that compared with full-sized hi-fi or monitor speakers, you won't be able to hear bass frequencies very clearly.

So-called 'powered' or 'active' monitors are probably the ideal in terms of sound quality. These tend to be about the size of your average hi-fi speakers, so can be equally awkward to find a home for, but are powered from the mains rather than via a separate amplifier. Cheap models from the likes of Behringer, Alesis, Samson, ESI Pro and M-Audio cost about £200, but you can spend thousands if you want. You'll get what you pay for. And whether you choose hi-fi speakers or active monitors, you'll benefit hugely from having them properly positioned, on proper stands, in a decent acoustical environment.

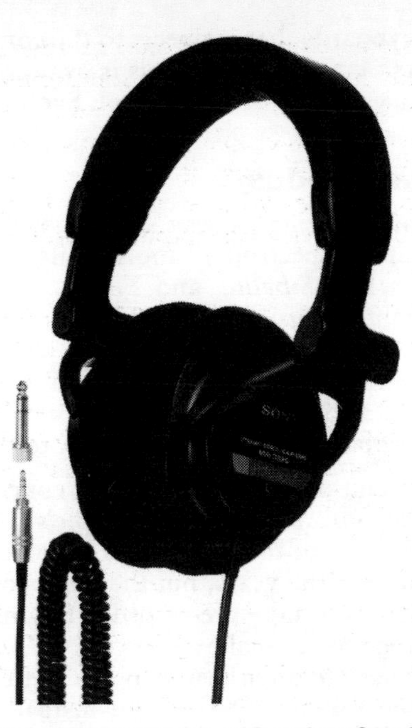

Figure 2.9 a good-quality pair of headphones, such as these Sony MDR 7509HDs, is almost essential if you want to create and record music on a computer

What else should be on your shopping list? Well, the chances are you'll want to upgrade the soundcard that comes with your computer before too long, but this is another problem we'll deal with in Chapter 08. For the time being, as long as your computer provides a way to turn off its own loudspeakers and plug in one of the alternatives just described, it'll do to be going on with. Similarly, unless you're happy to make instrumental music, you'll probably want a way of recording your singing onto the song. Again, this is something that will be discussed in detail in Chapter 08.

Finally, a keyboard – of the musical variety – is very useful when you're working with a computer. Even if you've never had a piano lesson in your life, you'll want a musical keyboard as a way of entering musical information into your software. Most of the varieties of electronic keyboard we've already examined will let you do this, but some – especially older ones – will need an extra piece of hardware called a MIDI interface. If developing your keyboard skills is not high on your agenda, you could get one of the many affordable and compact 25- or 37-note controller keyboards that connects to the computer directly, via its USB ports. A variety of models is available for under £100 from companies like M-Audio, Edirol, Evolution and Novation.

Working with loops

Computers are amazingly versatile, and when it comes to music, there's a complete spectrum of tools available. At one end there are packages like *Sibelius* and *Finale*, which are aimed at classically-trained musicians. These programmes, in effect, are designed for the sort of composers who would otherwise write their music straight on to paper, in traditional dots-and-lines notation, with a sprinkling of Italian terms. If you can do that, you should probably take this book back to the shop now.

It's the other end of the spectrum that concerns us here, with software like Sony's *Acid Pro*, Apple's *Garage Band* and Ableton's *Live*. All of these packages have become increasingly sophisticated over the years, but the basic concept remains the same. The idea is to take pre-recorded fragments of sound and string them together to make a song. As we'll discuss later in the book, pop songs are often made up of short elements which get repeated over and over again. So, instead of having a real drummer or bass player play the same thing repeatedly, you can take a few short sections from a recording of drums or bass guitar, and 'loop' them, to much the same effect. The creative element in this style of music-making usually lies in combining loops in interesting or unexpected ways, and the programmes listed above help to make this possible. For instance, you might find that your bass loop is slightly faster than your drum loop, so they don't sound very good when played together: these programmes will let you change the speed of one or both so that they match. There are also lots of fun ways to switch bits of loops around, make them higher or lower in pitch, and so on.

Where you get the loops from is up to you. The origins of this technique lie in 'sampling' bits of other records, a technique which is still very popular, especially in urban music. An obvious example would be Eminem's 'Stan', which basically borrows the entire first verse from Dido's 'Thank You' as its chorus. A less obvious one would be Amerie's recent hit 'One Thing'. The drum track is based on a loop from a song by funk band the Meters, and the point here is not that you'd recognise the source of the sound, but that it's a great drum track, regardless of where it came from. If you get into sampling, be prepared to spend a lot of time in second-hand record shops.

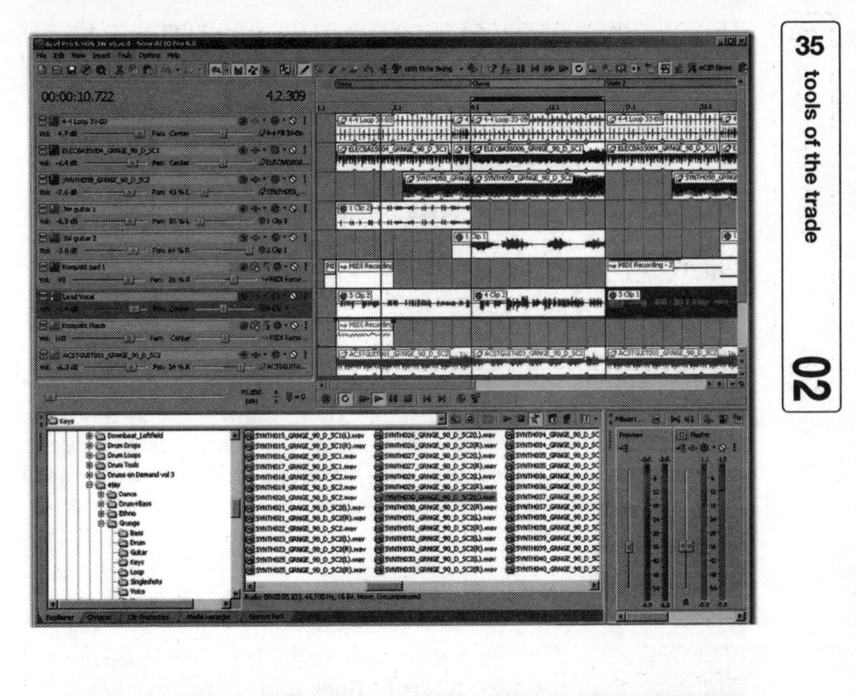

Figure 2.10 computer programs such as Sony's *Acid Pro* (top) and Ableton's *Live* (bottom) are designed to make music from 'loops'

The easy alternative is to buy ready-made loops. There's now a huge market in CDs and DVDs that contain nothing but hundreds of short snippets of drummers, guitarists and keyboard players doing their thing, intended precisely for use with the programmes described above. Because they're designed with this and only this in mind, they're usually a lot easier to work with than samples taken from 'real' records or CDs. You can, moreover, use them without running into problems over copyright, which will certainly rear their heads if you try to release a track that uses samples from other records. The negative aspect of this is that it's harder to come up with something really original or fresh-sounding when all you're doing is putting together loops from a CD called *House Anthem Construction Kit* or similar. In exactly the same way as tends to happen with the 'arranger keyboards' discussed earlier, it's all too easy to end up working with someone else's idea of music, rather than your own.

Mixing and matching loops can get you a long way, but in the end, if you want to be a songwriter as opposed to someone who makes instrumental dance music, you're likely to want to add something that you can't buy anywhere: a tune and some words of your own. All of these programs make it possible, assuming you have the necessary microphones and so forth, and we'll explain what you need to do this in Chapter 08, along with other kinds of recording software that are available.

Garage Band comes free with Apple computers, but isn't available for Windows PCs. By contrast, the full versions of the other programmes mentioned cost several hundred pounds, but it's worth pointing out that many soundcards and controller keyboards come bundled with slimmed-down versions of *Acid* or *Live*. Since you're likely to want to upgrade your soundcard and buy a controller keyboard anyway, this can be a good way to get started and find out which one is for you.

Other songwriting tools

The wonders of modern technology are one thing, but let's not forget a few simple items that can make a huge difference when you're writing a song. Obviously, you'll need something to write with and something to write on, but what may not be so obvious is that inspiration doesn't always strike when you have something handy. It's amazing how often a brilliant idea hits you at an inconvenient moment, and it's also amazing how swiftly those ideas can vanish from your mind. Carry a notebook so you can write them down, or a Dictaphone so you can sing them to your future self. Perhaps your mobile phone can be used for this purpose. If so, use it.

Finally, it's worth mentioning rhyming dictionaries, which some people find useful in the process of writing lyrics. Others don't. Try not using one to start with. Printed rhyming dictionaries are pretty cumbersome to use, and also incomplete – for instance, they don't contain multi-word rhymes. The best rhyming dictionary available is a computer programme called *Masterwriter*, but at nearly £150, this is a luxury most songwriters won't need.

hooks

In this chapter you will learn:

- **what we mean by a hook**
- **why hooks are fundamental to songwriting**
- **how to recognize a potential hook**
- **some techniques for generating ideas**
- **how to begin to develop those ideas.**

What makes a song memorable? Without thinking, most people would probably say 'a catchy tune', but there's more to it than that. Let's suppose you're listening to the radio and you hear a song for the first time. What would make it stand out? What would make you remember it?

Unless you're Mozart, chances are that the entire tune won't lodge in your brain the first time you hear a song. If you remember anything, it's more likely to be a small fragment of the song that's particularly arresting. And you're more likely to remember that fragment if it gets repeated lots of times in the one song, or if the structure of the song somehow makes it particularly prominent. What's more, that fragment might well not be a 'tune' at all. It could be a distinctive sound, or a strange word, or a neat little guitar riff.

The buzzword in the music industry for the fragments that make a song stand out is 'hooks'. And a hook can be almost anything. Let's look at a few examples of hooks from songs that became huge hits.

The Prodigy's 'Firestarter' does't really have a tune at all, but it's still an incredibly memorable record. The obvious hook is Keith Flint's repetition of the phrase 'I'm a firestarter... twisted firestarter'. Why should that stand out? He doesn't have a beautiful or even a particularly powerful voice, but he manages to put across that line in a way that's incredibly distinctive. It's partly his Essex accent, partly the venom with which he says the words, and partly the choice of words themselves – how many other songs are there that use the word 'firestarter'? In other words, it's the way it sounds that makes it stand out. That might seem stupid and obvious, but there's a point to be made: it's a fine example of a record that has a killer hook even though it doesn't have a catchy tune.

James Blunt's 'You're Beautiful' is the kind of record where you can sing along with the chorus the first time you hear it. On the other hand, few of us can remember any other parts of the song, even though we've all heard it a million times. So what makes that chorus so special? The tune, such as it is, is very basic: it's hard to imagine that we would all have it going round in our brains if it was played on a piano. There are two reasons why it's so memorable. One is that it gets repeated over and over and over again. The other is that, once again, Blunt's vocal delivery is really distinctive. There's something about the sheer noise he makes that sticks in the mind: it might sound like he's swallowing his tongue, and desperately trying to stretch the word 'beautiful' over more syllables than it really has, but the results are nothing if not unique.

What made Radiohead's 'Creep' such a big hit? Two things hit you when you hear it for the first time. One is the audacious chorus lyric 'I'm a creep / I'm a weirdo'. Regardless of the tune, that's a pretty powerful and shocking statement to hear from any singer. The other is the short, sharp bursts of noise from Johnny Greenwood's guitar. They're not even recognisable as notes, let alone a tune, but their sheer unexpected violence grabs your attention and won't let you go.

More conventional instrumental parts quite often overshadow the actual tune to become the most prominent hook in a song: think of the saxophone in Gerry Rafferty's 'Baker Street', the piano in Coldplay's 'Trouble', the cowbell rhythm at the start of the BBC's cricket theme, the bass line to 'Walk On The Wild Side', the guitar riff that opens 'Smells Like Teen Spirit'. For another example, take New Order's 'Blue Monday' – Bernard Sumner's glum, deadpan singing voice is one memorable feature: with its couldn't-care-less quality, it contrasts starkly with other pop records, which usually compete for your attention by being ever more chirpy. The most surprising hook in the song, though, is its machine-gun-like synthesized snare drum roll. It has no tune and no words. It's just one sound, repeated over and over again, yet it's the first thing that grabs you when you listen to the track.

It's even possible for total silence to be a hook: listen to Steve Harley's 'Make Me Smile' for one example.

Another kind of hook that's becoming ever more important in pop records is what you might call the 'production hook'. Sometimes this just means a clever gimmick, such as the digital vocal treatment that made Cher's 'Believe' so annoying, or the putting-the-record-through-the-tumble-drier effect on Lou Bega's 'Mambo #5', but these days, production hooks are central to the art of songwriting, too. Lots of modern hits are based on 'samples' taken from old records, where a short section of a record is isolated and used as the basic hook for a new song. This is often derided as lazy and unimaginative – by people who've never actually tried to do it. In fact, there's a huge amount of skill and artistry in listening to a record and pinpointing a potential sample. The best hip-hop and dance producers can bring out hooks that even the musicians who made the original records might never have noticed, or they can put together two or three samples that aren't necessarily catchy on their own, but fit together perfectly to create a hook. Some of those producers come up with great songs even though they can't play a musical instrument, such as the guitar or piano, at all.

Let's think again about the idea of a catchy tune. If, by that, we mean a sequence of notes that can be written down and plinked out on a piano – a melody, in theory-speak – it would be a mistake to think that catchy tunes are the be-all and end-all of songwriting. Many great songs have catchy tunes, but a catchy tune by itself won't make a great song.

Exercise

Listen to music radio for an hour or so. At the end of each song, make a note of anything about it that has stuck in your mind, whether that's a chorus lyric, a guitar riff or whatever. When you've finished, go back to your notes for the songs that came on earlier. Have any of the hooks you listed straight away stuck in your mind, and if so, which ones?

When it comes to writing songs, we need to cast the net wider. Thinking purely in terms of notes is too limiting, and puts us out of step with the modern music business. It ignores the importance of words, but more importantly, it ignores the fact that it's how things sound that matters. Even the songs that we think of as having catchy tunes usually stick in our minds partly because they're recorded using interesting sounds to play those tunes.

So what is it that makes some sounds into killer hooks and others not? One thing should be clear from the examples we've looked at – there's no magic formula for creating hooks. The most brilliant musicians in the world can fail where school kids in a garage can succeed. However, we can improve our chances of finding them by considering the resources at our disposal. Some of us have musical instruments, such as the guitar or piano. Some have computers, with their ability to record sounds, chop them up, repeat them and layer them. And we all have our voices. Those are the obvious things, but the most important resource for songwriting is our minds. We're all full of potential hooks: it's just a question of learning how to identify them.

Listen to tracks 1–4 on the CD.

Finding a vocal hook

The vocal line is the central part of nearly all great songs, so a good way to begin a song is to generate something that can be a sung or spoken hook. As we've seen, other kinds of hook can be important too, but it's pretty rare for a song to be a big hit if it doesn't feature the human voice doing something memorable or distinctive. To start with, let's come up with some words. We're not looking for an entire poem, or even a rhyme: just some short phrases that stick in the mind.

A hook can come anywhere in a song, but when we're talking about the words, there are two areas that are especially important. The opening line of a song is where the listener meets the singer for the first time. If we can engage the listener's attention straight away, the battle is more than half won. That can mean surprising the listener, impressing them, moving them, making them curious, shocking them or making them laugh. It can involve making a statement, asking a question, setting up a story or introducing a character. As a songwriter, you sometimes have an idea for the whole song in mind when you begin, so you know in advance what it is that you want the first line to do. However, at other times, a striking opening can be the spark for the whole song.

The other crucial line in most songs is the one that is, or that contains, the song's title. Rarely, a song is a hit that doesn't use the title as a lyric at all, but usually, it has a pretty fundamental part to play. If there's a chorus, it's almost always part of that, meaning it gets repeated several times, and is part of a musical climax. The title line can be the pay-off to a story or joke. It can summarise what went before, but it can also undercut what went before, turning it on its head. It can be a release of tension or the final tightening of the screw. It can be a shout of joy or the final nail in a coffin. Whatever it is, though, it has to be memorable, whether in its own right or because of how it relates to the rest of the song.

There are lots of ways to begin writing a song. You might start with a message that you want the song to put across, or a situation you want to describe, or an emotion you want to express. You might begin with a hook that doesn't involve vocals or words if you feel you've come up with an ear-catching arrangement of loops in a computer programme, or a guitar riff that has potential, or a nice arrangement of piano chords that's ripe for development. However, not all songs have to have a memorable riff, and at the start, we don't always have a clear idea of what we want every song to say: but all songs need to have a title and a first line, so let's think about starting with these.

If you do have an idea in mind for what you want the song to say, it's not a bad idea to spend some time thinking of a title that really sums up that idea. One way to do this is to think about your song as one side of a conversation, whether it's with someone in your life, the wider world, from a film or book, or a character you've invented. The best line in that conversation – the final verbal blow that puts the unfaithful lover in his or her place, the killer point that wins the argument – could be the line that makes your song.

Even when you do have ideas for songs, though, it isn't always easy to find the sort of memorable, pithy summing up that would make a suitable hook. On the other hand, if you have a killer hook, at least you have something concrete to build on in writing a song. So let's find some ways of generating those hooks.

Here are some ideas to get you started:

- Take a hook from someone else's song, and think of ways it could be turned on its head. For instance, 'I'm a weirdo' from 'Creep' could become 'I'm not a weirdo', or 'You're a weirdo', or 'I'm normal', or 'Am I weird?'.
- Take a hook from another song and imagine the question that that hook might be an answer to.
- Steal a line from a film or book, or an advertising slogan.
- Think of important conversations you've had, or letters or emails you've received: what was said to you that made a big impression?
- Imagine you're placing a personal ad. What would you write?
- Dip into a dictionary of quotations, or a list of well-known phrases and sayings.
- Try describing someone you know well in a single sentence.
- Buy a set of those fridge magnets with words on and rearrange them until you get something interesting.

Exercise

Watch an episode of a typical soap opera such as *Eastenders* or *Coronation Street*. Try to pay no attention to the plot: instead, think about each line in isolation as the actors speak them. Write down any lines that particularly grab you. When it's over, take a look at the lines you've written down and ask yourself whether any of them might be used in different circumstances. Who else might say them, and to whom?

Listen to tracks 5 and 6 on the CD.

Developing a hook

If all's gone to plan, you should now have some little pieces of song in front of you. Not everything you come up with will be suitable: indeed, you might end up throwing nine out of ten ideas away, but you have some starting points. So how do we go about turning a fragment of a lyric into a full-blooded song? Again, there are probably a number of approaches. Some people write the entire lyric before even thinking about setting it to music. Others can take the opposite approach. In both cases, the obvious pitfall is that you can end up with music and lyrics that don't quite work together. As we'll see later on, a good fit between words and tune depends on a lot of factors, many of which are quite subtle. When you come up with a tune by humming wordlessly, or by playing around on a musical instrument, it's surprising how often you end up with something that's completely unusable, simply because no words seem to fit it. Likewise, working with dummy or nonsense lyrics when you're writing a melody can be a problem, because it often turns out that no 'real' lyrics seem to fit as well as the gibberish you started with.

By starting with a real phrase or sentence, you make things simpler for yourself later on in the process. If there is a tune that fits naturally to your first line, chances are that other combinations of words will also work with that tune, which will make it easier to write the other verses or choruses of your song. If there isn't, at least you can abandon it at an early stage, before you've invested too much effort in it.

How can we tell whether a lyrical fragment holds any promise as the germ of a song? You can start to find out by simply saying it to yourself – ideally out loud, if you don't mind strange looks from fellow passengers on the tube. Is it easy to say? Is it satisfying to say? Or do you find yourself tripping over the words? Let's take a pair of examples from randomly chosen book titles: the phrases 'darker reflections' and 'building with straw bales'. The former feels pleasing to say out loud: the different sounds that make up the words follow naturally from one another. The latter, by contrast, is awkward and unsatisfying to say. The transition from the word 'with' to the word 'straw', in particular, is uncomfortable and requires effort to enunciate clearly. (Most people encounter a similar situation when contemplating names for their children: some first names fit naturally with their surname and trip comfortably off the tongue, while others tend to make you stumble.)

Assuming you've found a line that seems pleasing to say, the next step might be to think about the sounds that make up that phrase or sentence. English words are broken down into shorter units of sound called syllables. The word 'syllable' itself, for example, has three syllables which sound like 'si', 'la' and 'bull'. English is also what's called a 'stressed' language. This means that in any spoken (or sung) sentence, some syllables or words will be emphasized by comparison with the rest.

Stressed out

The same sentence can sometimes fit more than one pattern of stresses, and which pattern you use can change its meaning. For example, the simple sentence 'She ate the cake' can mean slightly different things depending on whether the word 'she', 'ate' or 'cake' is emphasized: that she, rather than someone else, ate the cake; that she *ate* it rather than doing something else with it; or that she ate the *cake* rather than something else.

Whether or not a phrase or sentence feels good to say out loud depends on the pattern of syllables it contains, and which of those are stressed. The key to fitting a lyric to a tune lies in identifying those patterns. In case this all sounds overly academic or scientific, don't worry: it's really a roundabout way of describing a process that will probably come naturally, if not straight away then soon. As ever, it's easier to do than it is to write about.

All syllables contain a vowel sound, flanked on one or both sides by consonants. The most fundamental difference, at least for our purposes, is between long and short vowel sounds.

Long vowel sounds

- 'ee' (cheese, feet, neat, Louise)
- 'ew' (you, lose, fluke, news)
- 'ah' (cart, dark, blah, star)
- 'ay' (rise, eye, fly, cries)
- 'oh' (joke, blow, slow, tone)
- 'ou' (pouch, ounce, doubt, out)
- 'er' (jerk, purse, fern, curt)
- 'or' (fort, caught, sport, poor)
- 'oy' (boy, toy, spoil, joy)

Short vowel sounds

- 'a' (black, cat, man, pad)
- 'e' (left, said, neck, tent)
- 'i' (hitch, lift, pick, sit)
- 'o' (cop, pot, wrong, lob)
- 'u' (muck, bun, tug, cut)
- 'oo' (book, cook, look, hook)

You can also distinguish different types of consonant sounds. Some are hard-sounding and snappy, like the 'k's in 'kick', the 't' in 'tap' or the 'p' in 'pot'. Others are softer, such as the 'th' in 'then', the 'sh' in 'shoes' or the 'v' in 'view'.

Let's make a first attempt at turning the lyrical fragments we've written down into musical hooks. When you sing, there's a low note you can't easily go below and a high note that you can't go above without straining. The space between the two is called your vocal range. Pick a note that's roughly in the middle of yours, leaving you room to go in either direction, and try singing the first few words of your chosen phrase on that note. Experiment with different timing, making some syllables long and others short. Experiment with singing some syllables loudly and others less so. You'll find that long vowel sounds can be stretched out, but short ones can't; and you'll probably find that the syllables that are naturally stressed in speech are the ones that feel most satisfying to emphasize when you're singing. The idea we're working towards is to work out what natural qualities your potential hook has, and exaggerate them, in the same way that a caricaturist might notice someone's bushy eyebrows and give them a huge sprouting forest of hair.

If you now have an idea about which syllables to emphasize, and which ones can be lengthened, you have a rhythm for your hook, which means you're half-way towards having a tune for it. We'll take a slightly more detailed look at these concepts in the next chapter, but for the time-being, let's consider some practical ways you might complete the picture.

It's worth asking yourself whether there's one syllable in the hook that is emphasized above everything else. (Again, this could depend on the way you're speaking or singing it.) Assuming there is, one way of coming up with a tune for your hook is to think of that syllable as the peak of a mountain. Try singing your line again, starting from the same note as before, but this time, don't stay on that note: go up in whatever steps seem comfortable until you reach the stressed syllable that's the peak of your mountain, then head down again. Use the same pattern of long and short notes you already worked out. Repeat it a few times, varying the steps between the notes.

Does that have what it takes to stick in your brain? Depending on the length of the line and the pattern of stresses, it might work. If it doesn't, try a variation. Taking the mountain metaphor a bit further, pick out a couple of other stressed syllables in your hook and think of those as smaller peaks in a mountain range. Try variants of your tune, rising to these peaks and falling between them. Or turn the idea upside down and think of some or all of the stressed syllables as low rather than high points.

Of course, not all hook melodies fit this pattern, where the most heavily emphasized syllables are the high or low notes in the tune, but it's quite common. A simple example would be James Blunt's 'You're Beautiful': the emphasis falls on the first syllable of 'beautiful', which is also the highest note in the phrase. Of the songs we looked at earler, Radiohead's 'Creep' is another example: in the hook line 'I'm a creep / I'm a weirdo' the two most prominent stresses fall on 'creep' and 'weird', which are also the two highest peaks in this particular range of musical hills.

Listen to track 7 on the CD.

If your chosen phrase has what it takes to be a vocal hook, that should become clear fairly quickly, and if you have to struggle long and hard over it, chances are it won't work. Indeed, before long, you'll probably find that the processes of thinking of interesting, hooky phrases and thinking of catchy fragments of tune to set them to often merge into one, so that you're unconsciously rejecting non-musical lines before you even get to the stage of trying to make them musical. Later on, it's likely that you'll also find yourself linking the process of coming up with vocal hooks much more closely with the business of working out suitable guitar or piano parts, or patterns of sample loops, to accompany them: and it's that business we're going to turn to next. Once we can place our vocal hook in some sort of musical context, the foundations of our song will be in place, and we'll be in a position to build on them and create the rest of the song.

Before we can get down to that, though, we need to equip ourselves with some basic music theory. This book will avoid using the language of music theory wherever possible, but there are some key concepts that we need to use to explain the next stages of creating a song. Some people find the idea of learning music theory intimidating, but it needn't be: things like scales, chord sequences and key changes are in the music you listen to every day, so even if you haven't thought about music in those terms before, they shouldn't feel like concepts from another planet. To most people who listen to a lot of music, especially those who already play an instrument, the small amount of theory we're introducing will basically be providing a way of talking about things that are already familiar in practice.

We'll return to the hook, or hooks, we just created in Chapter 05. In the meantime, let's make sure we don't forget them. If you have a Dictaphone or similar handy, it's a good idea to record yourself singing any particularly choice phrases you've come up with, and you should certainly write down any lines you feel have potential. Unless you 'read' musical notation – in which case you can almost certainly skip Chapter 04 – it'll be hard to find a way to write down the notes and their lengths exactly, but you could try to at least use symbols to remind yourself where the tune goes up and where it goes down. You could even mark off the notes on a piece of string and arrange it in a shape that reflects the tune. And if you're up to speed with basic MIDI recording (of which more in Chapter 09), you could record yourself playing the tune from a keyboard.

04 basic theory

In this chapter you will learn:

- **what we mean by 'music theory'**
- **how much music theory you need to know to write songs**
- **what we mean by rhythm, melody and harmony**
- **what we mean by the 'key' of a song**
- **what a chord sequence is, and how to construct one.**

Music theory can sound pretty daunting, especially if you pick up an old-fashioned academic guide to the subject. In the world of theory, music is described using words like 'cadence' and 'counterpoint', and unless you grew up in Simon Rattle's house, the chances are that this language will seem alien. Fortunately, there are two pieces of good news, as far as we're concerned. The first is that all this elaborate language has evolved to deal with classical music, and lots of it is simply irrelevant to pop. If you want to write like Bach, you need to know what a fugue is. If you want to write like the Beatles, you don't.

The second piece of good news is that in fact, you probably know most of the theory you'll need to know already: you just might not know that you know it. If you listen to a lot of music, you'll have a good idea what a key change or an ostinato sounds like. Learning the words just gives us the tools to talk about these things. We'll need to use some of this language to explain ideas in this book, but not very much; and if you have any interest in music, you'll probably find that the language of music theory is just providing new ways of referring to things you're already familiar with. That's especially the case if you know how to play a musical instrument such as the guitar or piano.

What you'll need to know is as follows:

- What we mean by rhythm, melody and harmony.
- How the rhythm of a song is divided into bars and beats.
- How notes are named, and how they can be combined to create chords.
- The difference between major and minor chords.
- What we mean by the 'key' of a song.
- How to transpose a sequence of chords from one key to another.

It's worth repeating that even though terms like 'bars' and 'key' might sound unfamiliar, the chances are that you are already familiar with what they refer to. And if you've learned guitar or keyboards in any kind of formal way, you may well know all of this already: by all means skip to the second half of this chapter if that's the case.

A more advanced knowledge of music theory can be useful in pop and rock songwriting, but it's crucial to remember that theory is a resource that was developed for classical composers and musicologists. Pop and rock songwriting often breaks basic rules, and in theoretical terms, most pop and rock songs are incredibly basic compared to a Mozart sonata or a

Rachmaninov concerto. Yet at the same time, music theory doesn't give us the tools to really understand a pop or rock song. The most important thing about pop music is the way that it sounds. The song itself is inextricably linked to the way it's performed and recorded, and this stuff just can't be reduced to dots and lines on the page. Pop music is about hooks, and you can't always write down what makes a sound into a hook.

Rhythm, melody and harmony

Among the most basic musical terms are rhythm, melody and harmony. These are prime examples of things you almost certainly understand perfectly well already, but we'll describe them very briefly.

Every sound has a start and an end, which means it lasts for a certain length of time. So do gaps or 'rests', when an instrument or voice is not making a sound. You create a rhythm when you play sounds or gaps one after another, and their lengths are related.

Some sounds, like the ones your guitar or piano makes, have a musical pitch as well as a length. These sounds are notes. You create a chord when you play several notes at the same time, and you create a melody, or tune, when you play notes one after another. (This means that a melody always has a rhythm.) Each key on a piano keyboard represents a different note; likewise, the frets on a guitar mark the point where each string is divided into separate notes. The 'low' notes are the ones towards the left of the piano keyboard or near the headstock of the guitar. The 'high' notes are towards the right of the keyboard, or the frets closer to the body of the guitar.

At any given point in a typical pop song, there's one main melody that stands out: usually the singer's voice carries the main tune, but pop songs also contain lead guitar and keyboard lines, for instance. The other instruments that are playing different notes at the same time are contributing to the song's harmony. Harmony comes from all sorts of possible sources, from guitars strumming to violins sawing and backing singers doing their thing.

Pop and rock bands have at least one instrument, the drum kit, which is purely dedicated to making the rhythm of the song, and has nothing to do with melody or harmony. Other instruments produce all three. For instance, the bass guitar plays tunes, and the reason why they're not always very interesting ones is because their purpose is usually to create a harmony. Some instruments, like the guitar and keyboard, can play more than one note at once, meaning that they can play melodies and harmonies.

The different instruments in a band fit together like a jigsaw to create a piece of music. So, for instance, the drums might play one rhythm, and the strumming on the guitar might play a second rhythm. The result of adding the two together is to create a third rhythm that's more complex and more interesting to the ear. Likewise, the bass guitar, the piano and the violin might just be playing one note each, but together, they make a fuller harmony.

Exercise

Listen to some songs you like and think about what the different instruments are doing. Is there one instrument that plays chords, and if so, what is it? Is there an instrument, such as a bass guitar, that plays its own melodic lines? What happens in the gaps where there is no singing?

Listen to track 8 on the CD.

Bars and beats

A beat is a short rhythm that's repeated over and over again, and in fact, pop music used to be called 'beat music', because rhythm is so important to it. Confusingly, though, the word 'beat' also refers to a part of a rhythm. If you listen to any pop or rock track, you'll hear that it has a regular pulse that you can count along to. Almost invariably, you'll find that it seems natural to count 'one, two, three, four' over and over again. If that's so, then the song is said to have four 'beats' to the 'bar'. A classical musician would describe it as being 'in 4/4 time'. You don't need to know what that means, but you should know that there are a couple of other arrangements that are sometimes used in pop music. The most common is '6/8 time', which you would count 'one two three, two two three'.

If the song has drums in it, and you know what the different elements of the drum kit sound like, you'll often find that the basic drum track in a 4/4 song goes 'bass drum, snare, bass drum, snare'; the bass drum falls on the first and third beats of the bar, the snare on the second and fourth. Other instruments in the kit, such as hi-hat and ride cymbals, might play on and inbetween those beats. In a 6/8 track the commonest pattern would be 'bass drum, hi-hat, hi-hat, snare, hi-hat, hi-hat', or something similar. Important musical events in a song, like a change from one chord to another, most often happen at the start of a bar, or half-way through one.

The idea that songs can be divided up into regular, repeated bits is another one you almost certainly understand already, even if you aren't familiar with terms like 'bars' and 'beats'. Likewise, you'll know that some songs are faster than others, but if you're making music on a computer, you also need to know that the speed of a song is measured in beats per minute or 'bpm'. The 'loops' that you work with in programs like *Garage Band* or Ableton *Live* nearly always consist of an exact number of bars of music – most often one, two, four or eight bars. If two loops have the same bpm value, they might fit together. If not, you need to speed them up or slow them down until they do.

One other important rhythmic concept in pop music is the idea of 'swing'. A swung beat is a rhythm where the notes that fall inbetween the main beats are consistently 'late'. In a non-swung rhythm, anything that happens on the 'one and a half' is exactly half-way between beats one and two. In a swung rhythm, it moves towards beat two and away from beat one. The classic swung rhythm is the 'shuffle' beat beloved of 'rock and roll' acts. To hear how it works, compare the Beatles' 'Revolution', which is swung, with 'Lady Madonna' or 'Get Back', which aren't. Swing can vary from the gentle to the obvious. 'Revolution' is at the latter end of the scale: the note inbetween beats one and two is not half-way between the beats but two-thirds of the way towards the second beat.

Intervals, scales and chords

There are 88 keys on a piano keyboard, but there are only 12 notes altogether. It's a bit like one of those rare times you see several rainbows stacked on top of one another. As you look up from the horizon, you go through all the colours in the first rainbow; if you keep on going up, you'll see the same colours reappear in the second and the third. You could think of music in the same way. There's a basic palette of 12 notes, but this palette keeps reoccurring as you go higher and higher up the keyboard.

The basic span of 12 notes is known, for reasons we'll come to in a minute, as an octave, which is why keyboard instruments are

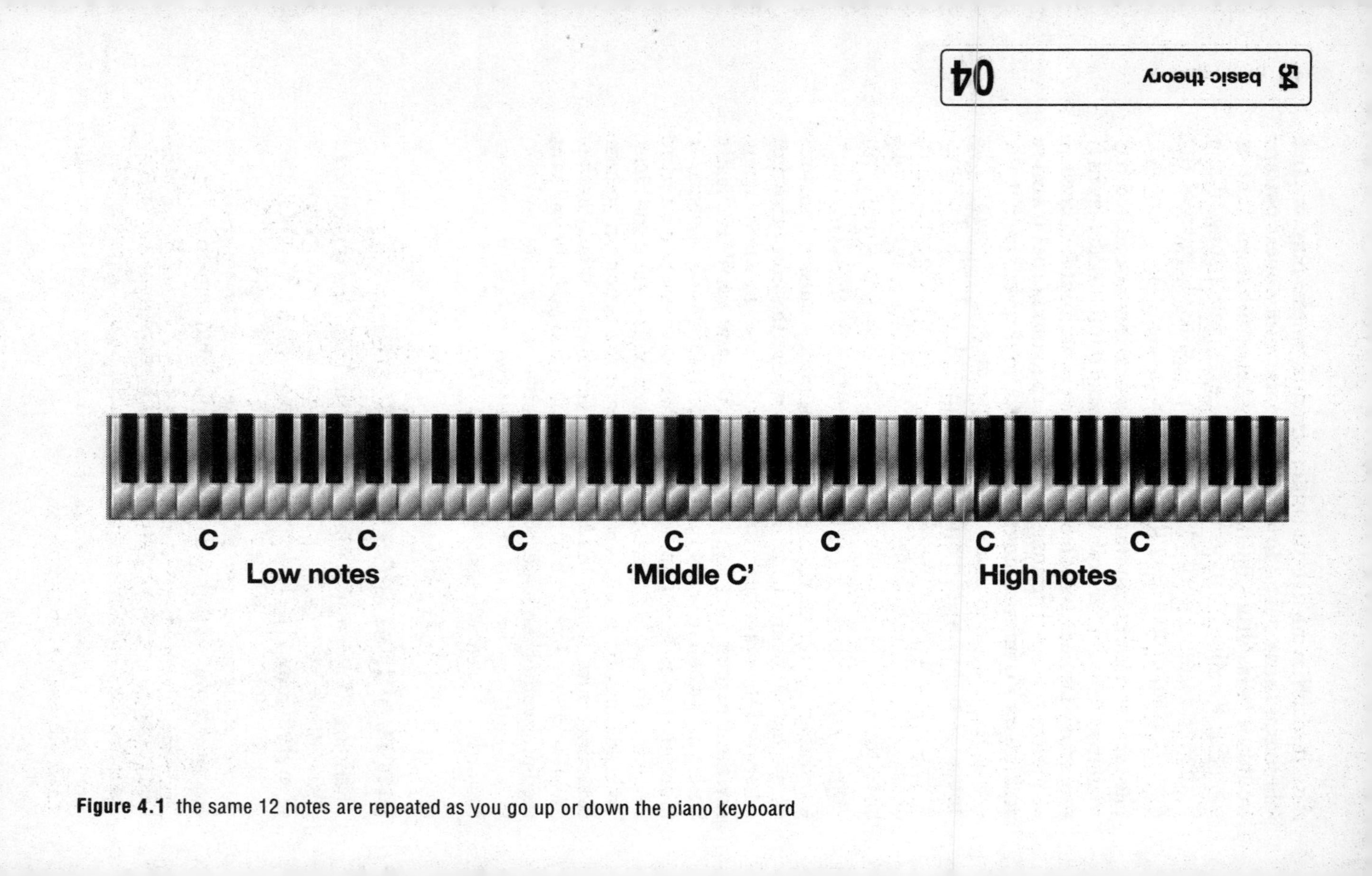

Figure 4.1 the same 12 notes are repeated as you go up or down the piano keyboard

described as having five- or six- or seven-octave keyboards. On a keyboard instrument, an octave contains seven white keys and five black keys. On a single guitar string, an octave spans 12 frets.

An octave is also the name given to the interval between a single note and the note 12 notes higher or lower. The two notes are separated by an octave sound recognisably the same, and they have the same name, but they're not identical: one sounds 'higher' than the other. On a guitar, the notes you get at the 12th fret, half-way along the neck, are an octave above the note of the equivalent string when it's not fretted at all (the 'open string'). The highest and lowest strings on a guitar are tuned two octaves apart.

You'd think that the obvious thing to do would be to give each of the 12 notes its own, fixed name and have done with it. Why not just use the letters A to L, for example? Unfortunately, music theory doesn't always appreciate the virtues of simplicity, and the 12 notes are named using the seven letters A to G, plus the words 'sharp' and 'flat'. If you look at a piano keyboard, you'll see that the plain letters name the white notes, while the names of the black notes can change. They can be referred to either as 'sharp' of the white key to the left, or 'flat' of the white key to the right. So, for instance, the black key inbetween G and A can be either a G sharp or an A flat. Which is it? Well, it depends. The rules are complicated, but the basic thing you need to remember is that sharps and flats don't mix. If there's one sharp going on, any other black notes playing at the same time are also referred to as sharps. (The words 'sharp' and 'flat' are not usually written out, by the way. Instead, the symbols # and ♭ are used, respectively.)

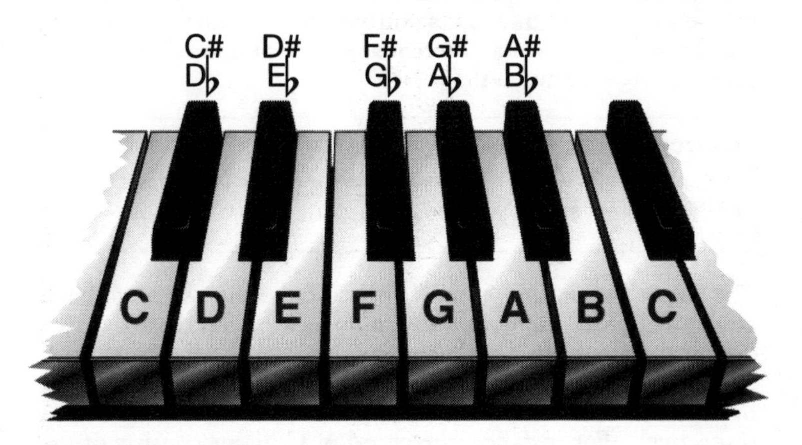

figure 4.2 how the notes are named

As well as the octave, there are some other intervals that are particularly important. The interval between two adjacent notes, such as C and C sharp, is called a semitone. Two semitones make a tone, such as between C and D. Two notes that are three and four semitones apart are known, respectively, as minor and major thirds. Five semitones make a fourth, and seven semitones make a fifth – the most important interval after the octave. So why don't we just call this interval a seventh?

Most of the time, music doesn't use all 12 notes in the octave. Instead, it relies on a selection, usually consisting of only seven notes (which is why the whole thing is called an octave: of the notes that are actually being used, the eighth is the same as the first). If you take a selection of notes from the octave and play them in order, up or down, the result is called a scale. By missing out different notes, you create very different musical characters. The most common scale is called the major scale. If you start it on C, it uses all the white notes on the keyboard and misses out all the black ones. And if you head up through the major scale, starting on C, the note G is the fifth one you arrive at: hence, though it's actually seven semitones above C, it's called a fifth.

There are lots of other ways of removing notes from the octave to create scales. The other one you're likely to encounter in pop music is the 'blues scale', one of several so-called 'minor' scales. As you can see in Figure 4.3, a blues scale starting on C differs from the major scale at two points.

What defines the major and minor scales is not a sequence of notes, but a sequence of intervals. So, for instance, the major scale consists of two whole tones, then a semitone, then three whole tones, then another semitone. If you start it on a note that's not C, you'll get a different sequence of notes, but with the same intervals between them.

Exercise

Pick a note at random on the keyboard or guitar, and try out some of the different scales you can make starting from that note.

The terms 'major' and 'minor' also describe the two most basic kinds of chord. You make a chord by picking out three or more different notes from a scale and playing them at the same time. Major and minor chords are what you get by picking out the first, third and fifth notes in the major and minor scales respectively. For instance, the chord of C major consists of the

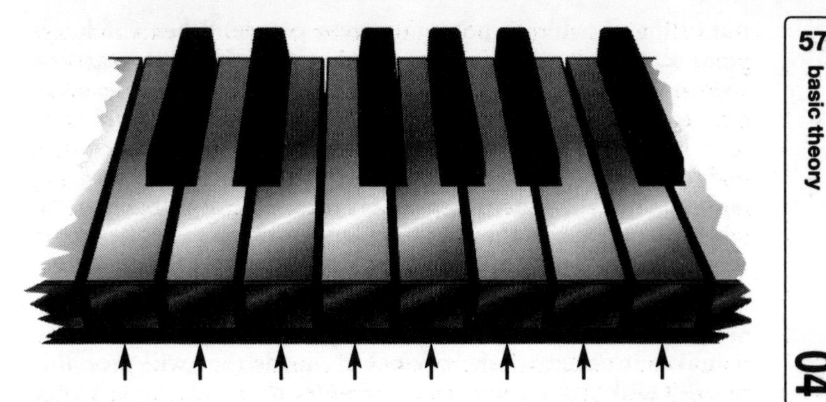

figure 4.3a the scale of C major uses only the white notes on the piano keyboard

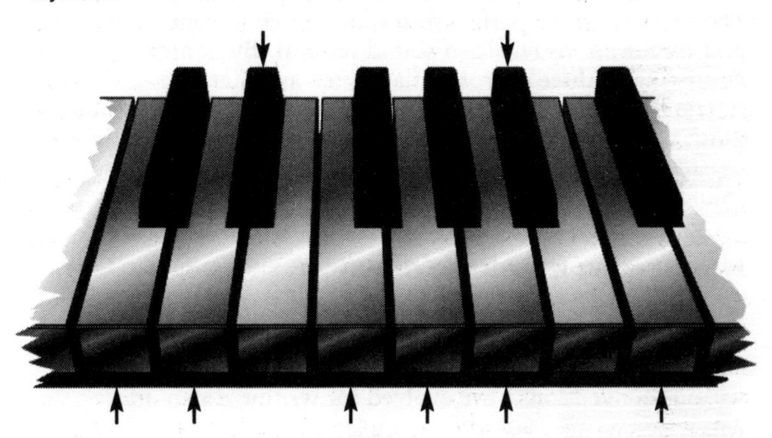

figure 4.3b the 'blues scale' in C differs from the major scale by using two of the black notes

notes C, E and G, while C minor is made up of C, E flat and G; the first note in the chord, such as the C in C major or C minor, is often called the 'root' note. Once again, we're describing something that you'll already understand if you play a musical instrument. (Note that chords as played on guitar or keyboards can include the same note repeated in different octaves. An open C major chord on the guitar, for instance, includes two Cs and two Es, each separated by an octave.)

The point of all this is that most melodies fit naturally into either a major or minor scale. In other words, it turns out that the tunes that come into our heads tend to use no more than seven out of the possible 12 notes in a given octave. When you know what scale the tune fits into, and what note that scale starts on (which won't necessarily be the same note that your tune starts on), you know the key of your song. You also have a pretty good idea what chords are likely to sound good as harmonies to fit with that tune. For example, if your melody fits most naturally with a major scale starting from G, your song is probably in the key of G major, and the chord of G major on guitar or keyboard would be a good starting point when you're trying to work out an accompaniment to it.

What's more, if you know that your song is in a particular key, it makes it easier to identify other chords that will probably 'work' with your tune. For example, the scale of C major contains the notes D, F and A. Together, these make up the chord of D minor, so this chord has the potential to be a pretty good fit with some part of your tune. Moving from a C major to a D minor chord will also sound natural. By contrast, a chord consisting of three sharps or flats, such as E flat minor (E flat, G flat, B flat) has nothing in common with the key or the notes in your song, so the chances of it fitting in are virtually non-existent; and following a C major with an E flat minor will sound jarring.

How music is written down

Sound recording is a relatively recent development in the history of music, but there's always been a need to preserve music so that it can be played and heard by other people. As a result, various conventions have evolved for writing down music.

When musicians talk about 'reading' music, they're referring to the system that will be familiar to anyone who's learned to play the piano, or any kind of instrument used in classical music. This uses five horizontal lines, or 'staves', with symbols that vaguely resemble the letters 'd' and 'b' placed on them to represent notes. You read the notes from left to right just like words on a page: the vertical position of the symbols tells you the pitch of the notes, while variations in their shape tell you how long they're supposed to be held for. Other symbols indicate rests (gaps), what key the piece is in, how fast it should go, and so on. It's a complete language for writing down music, and trained musicians can literally 'read' the shape of a piece of music from looking at it on the page. As you might expect, though, learning to read music is not trivial. If you have the opportunity to do so, you won't regret it, but plenty of professional songwriters can't, and you won't need to in order to understand this book.

figure 4.4 the scale of C major in classical notation

Guitarists may be familiar with a different system called tablature or 'tab'. This is similar in that it's designed to be read from left to right, but uses six lines, each representing a string on the guitar. Every note is written as a number, which tells you at which fret you need to hold the string down to produce that note. The main advantage of tab for guitarists is that it always tells you exactly which string to use to make each note, but this is more useful for learning other people's songs than it is for writing your own. This book does not use tablature.

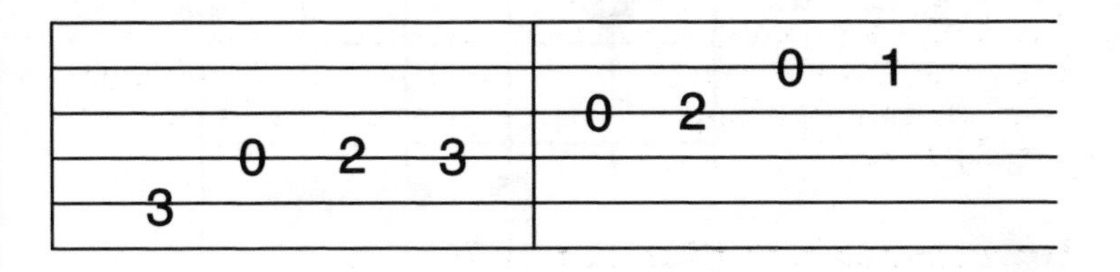

figure 4.5 the scale of C major in guitar tablature

Many songwriters these days don't bother writing down the melodies of their songs at all, preferring either to commit them to memory, or to record them. However, there is still a widespread need to write down chords: for instance, it'll make it a lot easier for other musicians to learn your songs if they have the chords to work from. The basic convention is that you write the chord name on its own (C, G, B♭, F#) if you mean the major chord of that name. If we want to indicate that a chord should be minor instead of major, we add a little 'm' thus: Am, Dm, C#m (C sharp minor), E♭m (E flat minor).

Most guitarists will also be acquainted with chord 'boxes', which tell you both the name of the chord and how it should be played. These can be useful, because most chords can be played in lots of different ways on the guitar, and you might want to specify a particular 'shape' for your song. The vertical lines in a

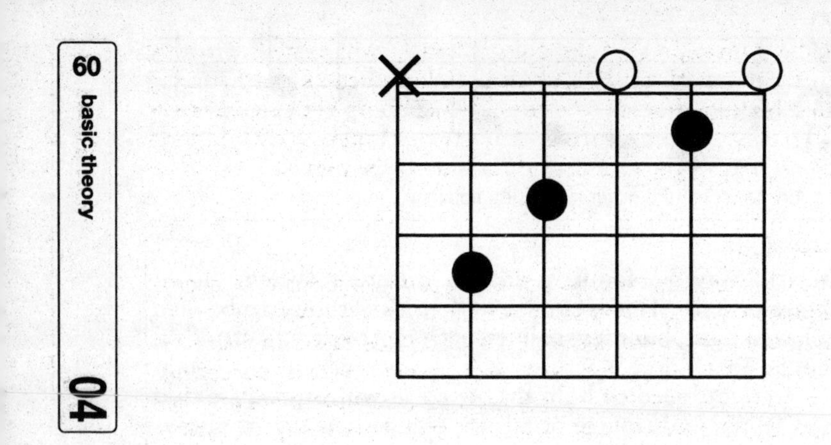

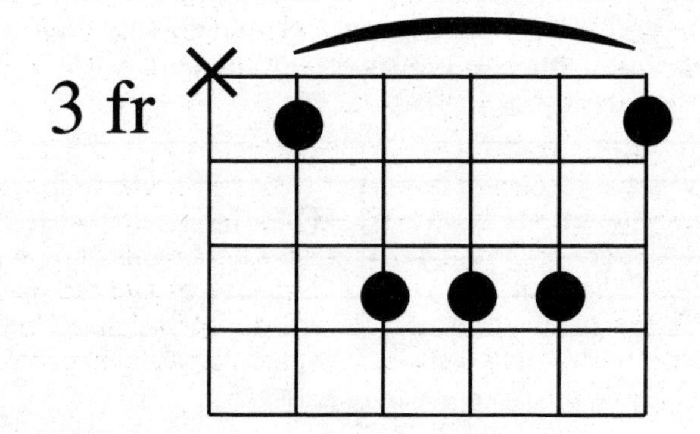

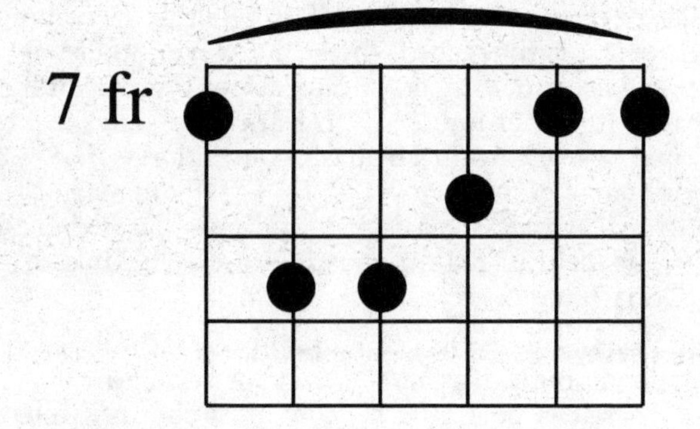

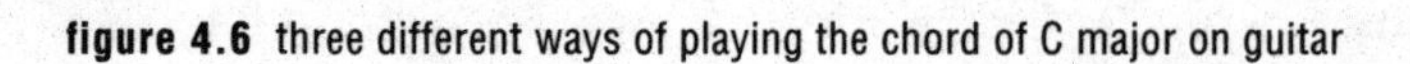
figure 4.6 three different ways of playing the chord of C major on guitar

box diagram represent the guitar strings, while the horizontal lines represent the frets. A solid circle indicates that a string should be fretted at that position, while an open circle instructs you to play the open string. Any strings marked with a cross form no part of the chord, and should not be played.

Inversions

When you're trying to work out a way to make a chord or chord sequence sound interesting on guitar, and especially on a keyboard instrument, it's a big help to understand the idea of inversions. We have described the chord of C major as consisting of a C note at the bottom, followed by an E note a major third above the C, and a G note which is a fifth above the C. However, we don't have to play the notes in that order. You could, for instance, rearrange them so that the C was an octave higher. This would make E the lowest note in the chord, but it wouldn't suddenly make the chord into an E chord!

What you've created by changing the notes around is the so-called first inversion of C major. As you can probably guess, the second inversion is the one where G is the lowest note. Both are still the chord of C major, but they have subtly different musical qualities. The first and second inversions of a chord are often described as being progressively less 'stable' than the 'root position' version of the chord. What this means in practice is that

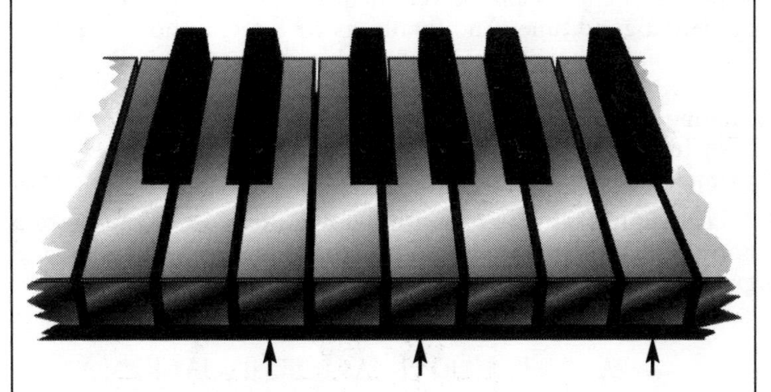

figure 4.7 when you play the chord of C major, but with E as the lowest note, the result is described as the 'first inversion' of C

they work less well as the starting point or final destination in a chord sequence. The second inversion is not that often used, but the first inversion offers a nice change of colour in the middle of a chord sequence.

When you see chord sequences for pop songs written down, inversions are usually noted by writing the chord name, followed by a slash and then the name of the lowest note. Thus the first inversion of C major would be written 'C/E'. Most pop musicians would describe this as being 'C over E', or perhaps 'C with an E bass'.

Chord sequences

A few tunes are so simple that the whole tune fits naturally against the same chord. If you listen to 'Pablo Picasso' by Jonathan Richman and the Modern Lovers, for example, you'll notice that the guitar simply plays an E minor chord throughout the entire song. However, most songs use more than one chord.

One of the most important aspects of songwriting is deciding which chords should follow each other, and when. It is important for several reasons. Most songs are incomplete without a set of chords to provide a harmony, and there are usually several different sets of chords that will work with any given melody. In the process of songwriting, thinking of a sequence of chords can be very helpful in inspiring you to come up with a good tune. And finally, as we'll see, a chord sequence can actually become a memorable feature of your song, especially if it's a bit unusual, or there's something fresh or exciting about the way it's played. From 'Wild Thing' to 'Smells Like Teen Spirit', lots of great records have been made great by a simple but effective sequence of chords on guitar or keyboards.

A fairly universal way of writing down the basic harmony to a pop song is to list the chord names that are used, in order, and give a rough indication as to how long each should be played for, in terms of a number of bars. For instance, you might write:

A | | | |D | |A | |E |D |A |

Each vertical line indicates the start of a new bar, and if no chord is indicated in a bar, that means we're still using whatever chord was last played. Remember, if we want to indicate that a chord should be minor instead of major, we add a little 'm' thus: Am, Dm, C#m.

What we've written down is an example of a chord sequence or chord progression. In this case, it's a very well-known chord sequence which actually has a name: the 12-bar blues. A fundamental feature of chord sequences is that you can isolate the sequence from the actual chords. In other words, the 12-bar blues doesn't have to start on an A chord: it can start on a C or an E or any other chord. All the other chords in the sequence would be different, too. What matters is that the interval between each chord name in the sequence is maintained. D is a fourth above A; E is a fifth above A, but a whole tone above D.

If you've got an electronic keyboard with a feature labelled 'Transpose', try this short experiment. Play three different chords in a row. Now Transpose the keyboard up or down by any amount you like (the manual should tell you how to do this), and play the same three chords. Notice how they now sound higher or lower, but the sequence as a whole still sounds the same. In other words, the effect of following an A chord with a D chord is just the same as the effect you get by following a C chord with an F chord. (If you play the guitar and you have a capo, you can try the same experiment. Play three 'open' chords without the capo, then attach the capo across any fret you like and play the same three chords.)

Nashville Numbers

Many songwriters who work in a conventional way using a guitar or keyboard find it helpful to think of chord sequences purely in terms of intervals. Instead of writing chord names down, they would write the 12-bar blues thus:

I | | | |IV | |I | V |IV |I |

This is called the Nashville Numbers system. It takes quite a lot of practice to work like this without having to continuously consult diagrams like the one we've used, but if you can, there are some advantages. If you write songs for other people, for instance, you often find that a chord sequence needs to be made higher or lower to fit with the range of notes they can sing. However, you won't need to learn the system in order to use the rest of this book.

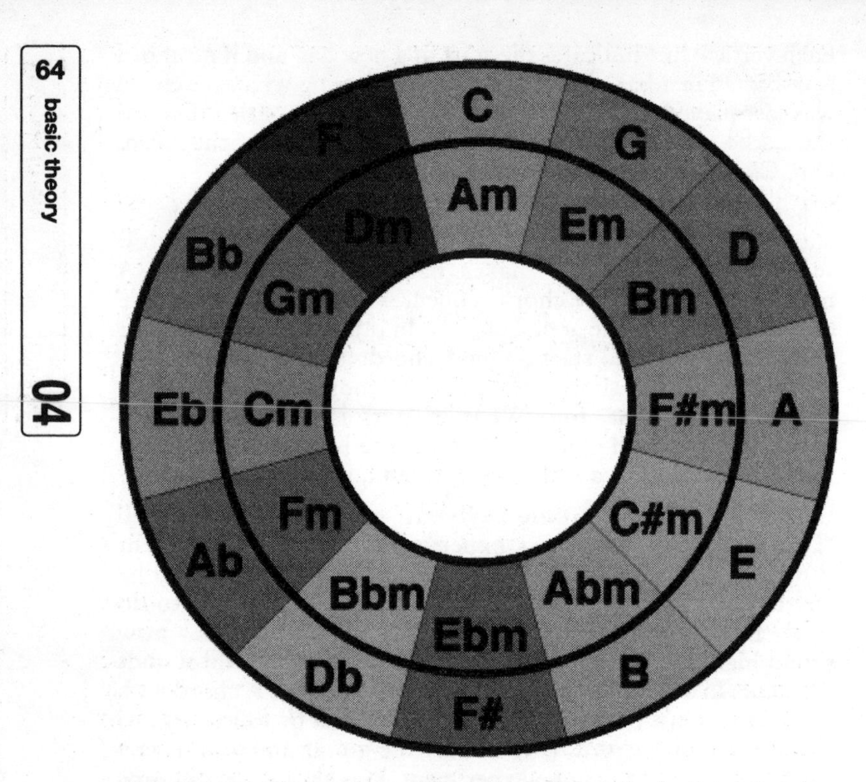

figure 4.8 This diagram shows all the major and minor chords. Chords that are close together are more closely related than those on opposite sides.

The diagram above shows all the major and minor chord/key names arranged in a circle. It's a diagram that is useful in lots of ways. One of them is helping you work out what the rest of the chords in a chord sequence will be if you decide to start it on a different chord. For instance, let's suppose we want to transpose our 12-bar blues so that it starts on a C. You'll see that you get from A to C by moving three steps anti-clockwise around the circle. To work out where all the other chords should go, just move them three steps anti-clockwise too. The result, a 12-bar blues in C, should look like this:

C | | | |F | |C | |G |F |C |

Note how the intervals are just the same: F is a fourth above C, while G is a fifth above C and a whole tone above F.

Exercise

Work out and write down the chords for a 12-bar blues in D.

Keyboard players will find that the 12-bar blues sounds very similar in every possible key, though it's harder to finger in some (unless you use the Transpose button!). Guitarists, on the other hand, will find that the sound of a chord sequence is a bit more variable, unless you depend only on a capo to move it up and down. For example, the 12-bar blues in A can be played using only open chords, but try playing it in E flat without a capo! If you ever wondered why all AC/DC songs are in the key of A, this should give you some idea.

A 12-bar blues in the key of A starts and finishes on the chord of A, but this isn't the case with all chord sequences, so don't automatically assume that a chord sequence is in the key of A just because it starts or finishes with an A chord.

If you're working with a software package like *Live* or *Garage Band*, and you buy a commercially produced library of loops to help you put your songs together, either the packaging or the filenames of the loops should list a key for each of them. Because the loops are likely to be very short, the key will also be the main chord that occurs in that loop. If you want to assemble a chord sequence, you can string together loops in different keys; alternatively, the programme will allow you to shift a single loop up or down in pitch, so you can create a chord sequence from a small number of loops.

As they're laid out in Figure 4.8, the chord and key that is closest to C major is A minor. The same goes for all the other major chords: the nearest chord in each case is the minor chord directly inside it. This is not an accident. The reason is that a minor scale starting on A contains almost exactly the same notes as a major scale starting on C. As a consequence, A is called the 'relative minor' of C.

If you're a guitarist or keyboard player, try the following experiment. Take a simple song you know that uses mainly major chords, and write down the chord sequence. Then use the diagram to work out the relative minor chord for each of those major chords. You should now have a chord sequence consisting only of minor chords. Now try singing the song to those chords instead. How does it sound? Chances are the tune will more or less fit, but it'll have a different feel to it: sadder, more reflective, or perhaps just plain depressing.

On a more cheerful note, if you've taken in all of the above, you now know enough music theory to read the rest of this book. So let's get to work on your song. How can we go about finding a musical backing that can support and enhance a vocal hook?

developing a hook

In this chapter you will learn:

- **how to find chords that will fit a vocal hook**
- **how to make the chords into an interesting musical backing**
- **how to begin developing this hook into a complete song.**

If you've followed the book so far, you should by now be equipped with three things. Firstly, a musical instrument, or a computer with suitable software for making music; secondly, one or more ideas for vocal hooks, each with words and a tune; and thirdly, an understanding of some basic concepts from music theory, including the idea of scales, chords and chord sequences. If so, it's time to begin putting the first and the third items on that list to work on the second.

Music theory can give us an idea of what to expect when we put different chords together, and it can explain why some things tend to sound 'right' and others don't, but it can't write songs for you. Knowing what key your tune is in, or what rhythm it has, won't make it a better or worse hook. That's why, in Chapter 03, we concentrated on getting things sounding right, without worrying about exactly why they did. If you do ever run into a situation where what your ears are telling you conflicts with what theory tells you, you should always follow the advice of legendary record producer Joe Meek: if it sounds right, it is right.

The ideas we discussed in Chapter 04 can't make a hook out of nothing: only your imagination and creativity can do that. However, what music theory *can* do is help you to develop the fruits of your imagination, turning fragmentary hooks into full-length tunes and finding the right musical backing to support them.

Sing back to yourself the vocal hooks you developed in Chapter 03. At the time, we deliberately avoided thinking of the musical elements of these hooks in theoretical terms, but if something came to your mind as being memorable, the chances are it fits into some theoretical ideas. We saw that phrases and sentences in the English language contain various kinds of sounds, some of which are naturally longer or shorter, and some of which are emphasized by comparison with the rest. And we tried to turn these phrases into musical hooks by fitting them to a tune that reinforced these natural properties.

Although we weren't thinking about the concepts of scale or key, it's very likely that the tune you found memorable fits into a common scale such as the major or blues scale. If you can pick out the notes on piano or guitar, you can probably work out which scale and key it's in. For example, a tune that uses only the white notes on the piano is likely to be in a key such as C major or A minor, and you can be confident that chords 'close' to those will be a good starting point. Even if you can't play your tune on an instrument, it should be easy enough to work out the chords that will fit. Sing your hook over and over again and play different chords underneath until you hit on the ones that work best. Likewise, if you're using a computer, experiment with different loops in different keys, or move a single loop up and down in pitch until you get a good match.

Like all melodies, the tune we came up with for our hook has a rhythm. And if it's a memorable hook, it may well turn out that part of what makes it so is a strong or interesting rhythm. When that hook is part of a complete song, there will be other elements that provide rhythm, too, but they all have to fit the main vocal hook; and a vocal hook with a strong rhythm often suggests a rhythmic feel for the entire song. In pop and rock music, it's often the case that just one repeated rhythm anchors the whole song, so it's vital that what you come up with fits the vocal hooks and is effective in its own right.

We saw that the most strongly emphasized syllables in a phrase often have particular importance in the tunes that fit that phrase, and the same goes for the rhythm of any musical backing that's likely to fit it. Stressed syllables 'want' to fall in musically significant places, especially the first beat of the bar. Think of the chorus to Blur's 'Girls And Boys'. All the emphasis is on the repeated words 'girls' and 'boys'; the former always lands on the first beat of the bar, the latter on the third beat (which is probably the next most important in a 4/4 song). Or take the first couple of lines of Roy Orbison's 'Pretty Woman': 'Pretty *wo*man / walking *down* the street / pretty *wo*man / the kind I *like* to meet'. Again, the most prominent stressed syllables, italicised here, fall naturally on the first beat of the bar.

We can turn this around to try to fit our hook to a musical backing. Think again about the most prominent point of emphasis in that hook, the peak of our mountain range. Pick out another couple of stressed syllables, if you can find them. Sing the hook over and over again, and on each of these stressed points, tap your foot or click your fingers. You should find that by filling in the odd gap, you can keep up a steady, unvarying tapping rhythm that fits naturally under your hook.

We've already found a chord that should work with this hook, so let's try experimenting with some different rhythms. If you're working with loops, most of them will already have a firm rhythm of their own, so the key is to find one that matches the hook. The first step is to get a handle on the speed of your song. One way to do this is to look for a function called 'tap tempo' in your software, if it exists. As the name suggests, what this does is allow you to tap out the beats of the bar on the computer keyboard, rather than on the floor. The software will calculate a figure in beats per minute (bpm) that corresponds to your tapping. Even if your software doesn't have a 'tap tempo' function, it should at least have a 'click' or 'metronome'. This plays back a simple percussive noise on every beat of the bar, so you can find the right tempo by changing the setting manually until the metronome matches your floor-tapping.

When you have an idea of the right tempo for your hook, you can then look for loops with similar bpm values; other loops that are much slower or faster can be sped up or slowed down, but the sound quality will suffer, and often the results will be disappointing. (One exception is that sometimes you can get good results by setting the tempo to half or double the calculated value and looking for loops close to that setting instead.)

Now set that loop to repeat over and over again, and try singing your hook over the top. If it's a simple loop without a complex rhythm of its own, the hook is more likely to fit. A more complicated loop might include lots of sounds occurring between beats as well as – or instead of – on the beat. Such a loop will be less versatile, but if you can find one that fits in with the ways your hook moves around the beat, it can do more to reinforce it. For instance, if your hook includes some words that fall between beats, a loop that echoes that pattern and matches the degree of swing would be perfect.

If you're using a piano or a guitar, you have to find a rhythm of your own. You might be able to get away with just playing the chord(s) over and over again on each beat of every bar, or each beat and half-beat – this has been quite popular in indie-rock circles over the last few years – but at other times, you'll want to complement your hook with something a bit more interesting.

On guitar, your basic options are strumming, picking and a combination of the two. Which one is right for your song will depend on lots of factors, including the style of music you want to make, the speed of the song and your own ability on the instrument. Lots of new songwriters fall into the trap of using the same one or two guitar rhythms on all their songs. The result is that although the songs can sound good on their own, they all tend to sound the same when played one after the other, such as at a gig or on an album. Whatever your level of skill, there should be enough variety of strumming and picking patterns available to ensure that this doesn't happen; and it's likely to be less of a problem if you use the approach described in this book, developing vocal hooks first and then trying to find guitar parts to fit them, rather than starting with the guitars.

Anyone who learns guitar will learn other people's songs, and you may also pick up generic 'licks'. Both are fertile sources of ideas for guitar parts. Try copying the strumming patterns from records in the style you want your song to have.

It seems to be accepted in pop music that guitarists can simply strum chords over and over again, if they want to, but for some reason, keyboard players need to offer something at least a little more sophisticated. Writing music for keyboards is a huge subject that's beyond the scope of this book, but there are a few simple ways to make a chord or chord sequence sound more interesting. One is to arpeggiate some or all of the notes in the chord. What this means is that instead of playing them all at once, you start at the bottom and work your way up, in time with the rhythm of the song. Another is to take advantage of the fact that you have two hands and use them to do slightly different things. The right hand could play the chord, while you play a simple bass line on the left hand: for instance, you can achieve an instant country and western feel by using the left hand to alternate between the root and fifth notes of a chord while the right hand plays the chord on the second and fourth beats of the bar. Alternatively, you could use the right hand to play something resembling the melody of the vocal hook, while the left hand takes care of the chords.

When you're trying to work out a way to make a chord or chord sequence sound interesting on guitar, and especially on a keyboard instrument, don't forget to think about how some of those chords could be inverted. In particular, inversions are a great help in coming up with an interesting bass line, or left-hand piano part, as it's the lowest note you play that determines which inversion is formed. For instance, consider the following chord sequence: C major, G major, F major, G major. What should the left hand play on the keyboard? If you want something more interesting than the root notes, try playing a descending scale from C: C, B, A, G. These notes will fit under the chords in the right hand, but they also form a more interesting left-hand part in their own right, and help to add some substance to the piano arrangement.

What we've done here is use the first inversion of the two middle chords in the sequence, by placing a B note at the bottom of a G chord and an A at the bottom of an F chord. Note that this

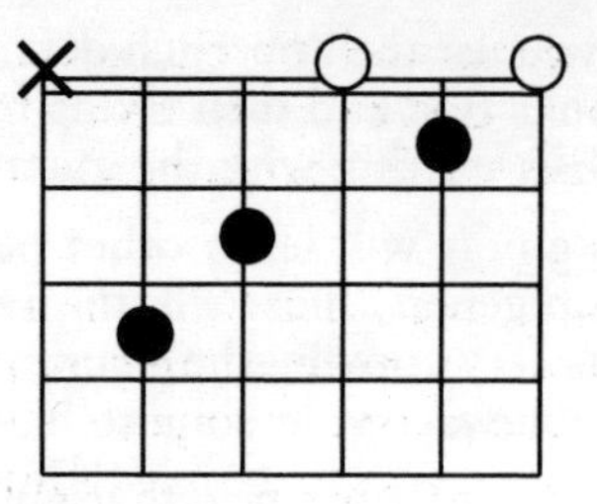

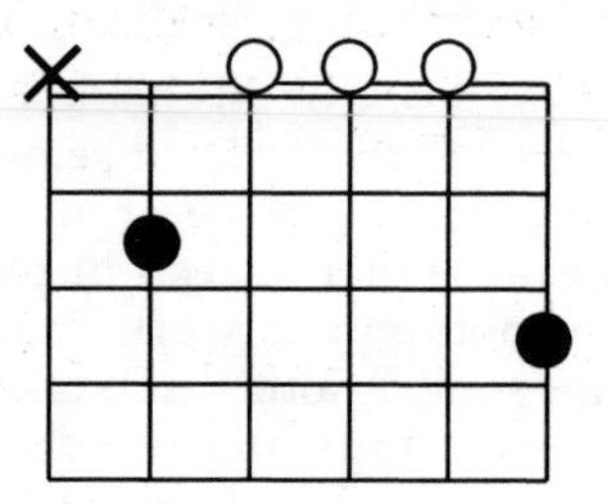

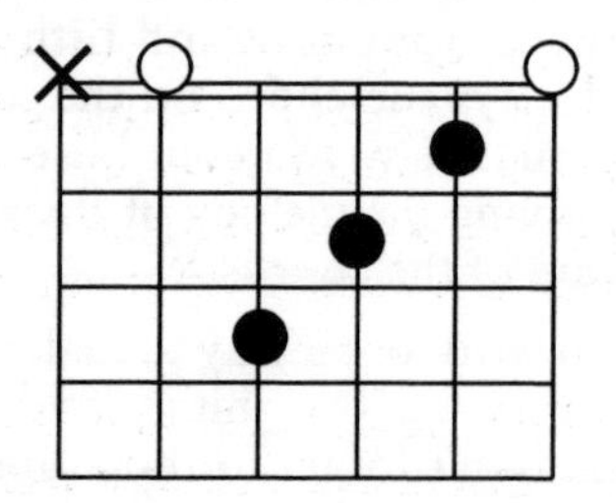

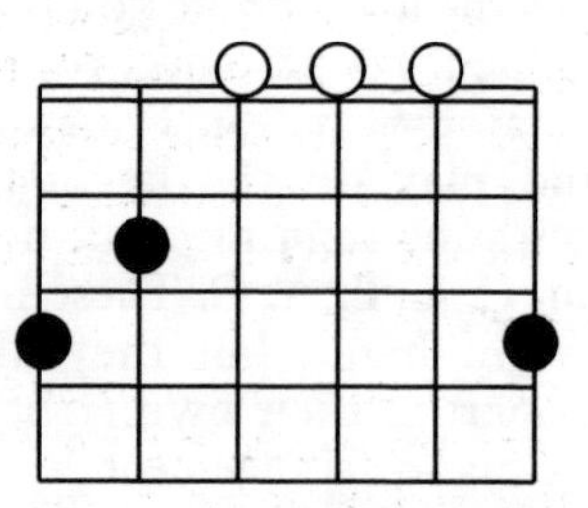

figure 5.1 You can often make a simple chord sequence more interesting by using different inversions to add a more memorable bass line. Here, the lowest notes in the four chords form a descending scale starting on C and ending on G.

particular example works well on the guitar, too. Instead of playing a conventional G chord, you can simply miss out the lowest G; and instead of a full, barred F chord, you can leave the A string open.

Another idea is to use a 'pedal note'. This is a single note that is maintained throughout a chord sequence, giving a sense of continuity through the chord changes. The guitar part to 'Wonderwall' by Oasis is a good example of this: the high G note played on the E string is kept going through all the chord changes. You'll often find that it sounds OK to keep a pedal note going even though it doesn't strictly belong to all the chords in a sequence. For instance, you could try playing a high or low D note all the way through this sequence:

Dm |C |Gm |B♭

Three of the four chords contain a D, and although the C major doesn't, you might find that in context, it sounds good, linking the chords on either side.

Choosing a chord sequence

If things have gone according to plan, you should now have found a chord that fits under your hook line, decided on a rough tempo, and come up with a suitable loop or a way of playing the chord on guitar or piano that provides a good rhythmic match for your hook. The next step is to develop that single chord into a sequence of chords.

Depending on how long your hook line is, and how many different notes it uses, you might find that it works perfectly well over a single unvarying chord. If the hook stretches over more than a bar or two, though, it can probably be broken down into shorter sections, each of which fits more naturally with a different chord; and even if the hook itself is happy sitting on a single chord, there's still the rest of the song to think about. In other words, now is the time to construct a chord sequence for our song, or at least for the part of it that includes the vocal hook we've been working on.

Again, you can do this by calculation or by trial and error. If you want to take the former approach, pick out the tune to your hook on piano or guitar and write down the notes. Then work out where it divides up into bars, consider the notes that fall into each bar, and look for the chord that is closest to including all of them. (There is, of course, no reason why chord changes always have to come at the start of a bar; nor do they have to happen in every bar.) For instance, if the notes of your tune are C, E, F, D, G, D, C, and it stretches across four bars, with the C, F, G and C falling on the first beats of those bars, a natural chord sequence might be C major (includes C and E), D minor (includes F and D), G major (includes G and D) and C major.

There are other chord sequences that would fit all the notes in that tune, but fitting the tune isn't the only consideration we need to worry about. In the short sequence listed above, each chord follows on smoothly from its predecessor, and the sequence as a whole reaches a natural conclusion with the transition from G major back to C major. By contrast, the chords of A minor, B♭ major, G major and A♭ major also fit with the four bars of our tune, but as a sequence, they sound jarring, or at best incomplete.

That doesn't necessarily make them bad: in the right hands, a sudden jump between two not-very-close chords can be a very effective songwriting tool. However, it's rare that a chord sequence consisting of a whole series of such jumps ever works. We saw in the previous chapter that most songs are based around a fixed selection of only seven notes out of the possible 12. This selection determines the key of the song, and usually a chord sequence will be based around chords that fit into that key. Indeed, a sudden jump to an unrelated chord is much more effective if the previous chord changes have established in the listener's mind a stable key for the song. By contrast, it's also possible to move smoothly between chords that are not at all close by choosing the right intermediate chords.

Let's take another look at the chord circle we met in the previous chapter. We can use this as a quick guide to see which chords are likely to work best in a given key: the further away any chord is from your key, the more jarring it will sound in that key. Similarly, you can use this diagram as an aid to guessing which chords will follow most easily from each other. Moving from one chord to its immediate neighbour will sound smooth and natural; suddenly jumping half-way round the circle won't. For example, the chords of B minor and B flat major are each only two steps away from C, so either may work in a song that's in the key of C. However, they are four steps apart from one another, so a direct jump between the two is unlikely to sound smooth whatever the key of the song.

The following list contains some of the most commonly used four-chord sequences in pop and rock music. Try following some

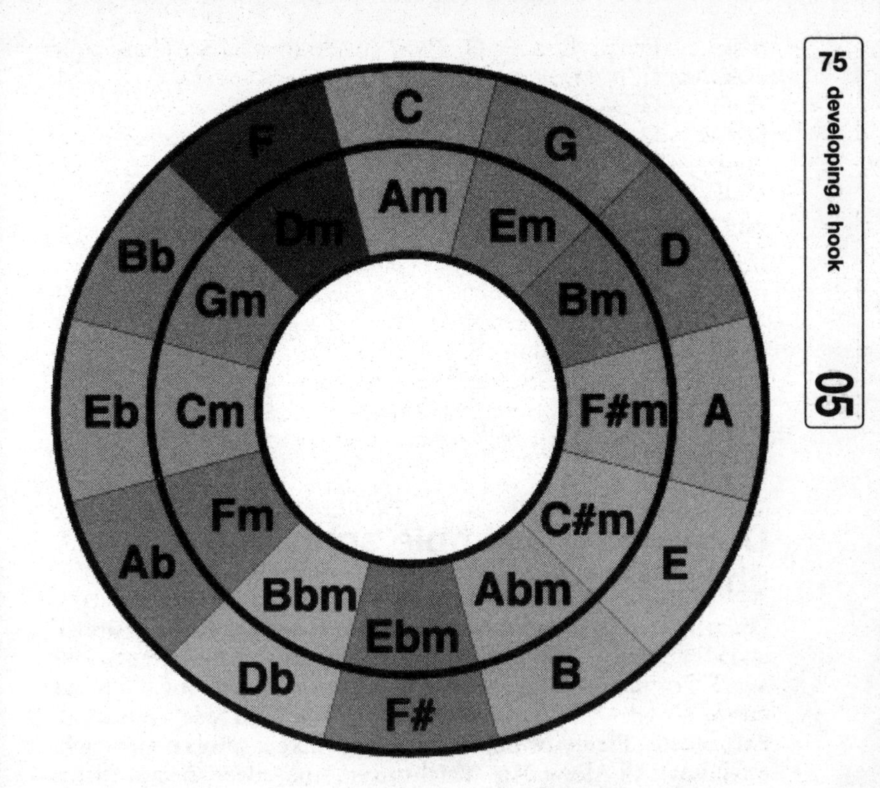

of them around the circle of chords to look at the transitions that are used (and by all means try stealing these chord sequences for your own songs!). These are all listed in the key of C major or A minor, but as we saw in Chapter 04, the circle diagram should help you transpose them into different keys.

C	Am	F	G
C	Em	F	G
C	Dm	F	G
C	Am	Dm	G
C	E	F	G
C	E	Am	F
C	E	F	Fm
C	G	F	Fm
C	F	G	F
C	F	G	C
C	F	Dm	G
C	F	G	Am

C	F	C	G
C	G	F	G
C	G	F	C
C	G	B♭	F
C	Bm	G	C
F	Am	G	C
F	Dm	G	C
Am	G	F	E
Am	F	C	G
Am	C	Dm	G
Am	G	C	F
Am	F	G	Am
Am	E	F	G
Am	Em	F	C
Am	Dm	G	C

Developing a simple song from a chord sequence

Quite a lot of pop and rock songs rely on one or two very simple chord sequences like those listed above, repeated over and over again. For instance, apart from one short section ('But she never lost her head...') Lou Reed's 'Walk On The Wild Side' consists of two chords. Plenty of Bob Dylan songs take a similar approach, including 'All Along The Watchtower', and unsurprisingly, it's a staple of punk rock – the Ramones built a career on it. Radiohead's 'Creep' is a more recent example of a song that just uses the same four chords over and over again.

If a basic chord sequence such as those listed above works well with your vocal hook, you could think about taking the same path. Simplicity is usually a virtue in pop songwriting, and if three or four chords are all you need to say what you want to say, there's no reason to use more.

Songs, or sections of songs, that are based around simple chord sequences usually feature quite a lot of repetition in the vocal line, too. They might not repeat the same words, but all the lines often have the same form, following the same melody and having the same patterns of stresses and long or short vowels. So if you have a vocal hook that works well, you can sometimes develop that into a song simply by coming up with 'more of the same': that is, by writing more words that fit into the same template.

The obvious risk with this approach is that you might end up with something so repetitive that it quickly becomes boring. The shorter the hook you're repeating, and the more times you repeat it, the greater the danger of this. Conversely, the more variation you can incorporate, the more interest you add.

For instance, if your vocal hook line fits well over just one chord, you may well find that for other lines in the song you can use the same tune but set it over a different chord. This is the basis of nearly all blues songs.

Rather than simply repeat your hook line several times in a row with variations to the words, you could also think about alternating it with a different line. Instead of having the first, second, third and fourth lines all the same, you could, for example, have the first and third the same, but the second and fourth be a different length or have a different pattern of stresses – and, as a result, a different rhythm. There are lots of other ways to combine lines that have varying lyrical features, and we'll look at this subject in more detail when we get onto rhymes and rhyme schemes in Chapter 06.

As well as varying the patterns of words across lines, you can also vary the tune. For instance, if you have what is basically the same line repeated four times, it can be an effective device to change the tune on the last repetition: try going up where the other lines go down, or vice versa.

Finally, of course, the fact that your hook is catchy enough to bear repeating doesn't mean it has to be the only vocal hook in your song. The sort of repetition we've described here could be used for just one section of the song, such as a verse or chorus. Another section could be derived from a different hook with a completely different melody, rhythm and chord sequence.

Going back to our roots

As we've just seen, the simplest way to create a song from a vocal hook line is to find a short chord sequence that fits underneath that hook line, then repeat it with minor variations to the words. Some classic pop and rock songs have been written that way, and back in the days of rock and roll, it was perhaps the norm. Since then, however, pop songwriting has tended to be more sophisticated, and even the most hardcore punk rocker is likely to feel limited if they stick to that method alone. We can probably thank the Beatles, among others, for the fact that pop and rock songs nowadays mostly use more complex chord sequences, and build complete lyrics from their vocal hooks in a more fluid, less repetitive fashion. This isn't necessarily better or worse, but it opens up lots of additional possibilities and allows us to exploit potential hooks that simply wouldn't work in a more basic musical context.

So how might we go about constructing a more complex chord sequence? Take another look at the array of common four-chord sequences listed earlier. You'll see that not all of these chord sequences begin or end with a C major or A minor chord: so what is it that makes them in the key of C major or A minor? Well, strictly speaking, most of these chord sequences could actually work in other keys too, if the context was established by other chords that came before them. In the simple case where these four chords are simply repeated over again, though, C major or A minor are the most natural keys, and one reason for this is that all these chord sequences naturally resolve onto the chord of C major or A minor. Let's take the first sequence in the list as an example: C Am F G. If your song consists of those four chords repeated over and over again, what happens when you want to finish the song? If you simply stop playing when you reach the A minor or the F or G major, the ending won't feel very final. It'll be as though something is hanging in the air, waiting for a resolution that only comes along when you get to the C major chord.

In many pop and rock songs, the moment where the chord sequence resolves itself onto the chord that expresses the key of the song is a musically important one. And it doesn't just, or always, happen at the end. In fact, in the example we've just looked at, the resolution happens every time the chord sequence cycles around. This means that the chord sequence is inherently satisfying and feels complete, even though it's so short. On the down side, though, it means that the impact of the resolution is pretty much diluted through constant repetition. In a chord sequence which stays away from the root chord for longer, by contrast, the resolution is likely to feel more dramatic when it does arrive.

There are various ways to delay resolving a chord sequence so as to make more of that moment. One is not to repeat the whole sequence, but a shorter section of it that doesn't include the root chord. In the example above, for instance, you could adapt the sequence to become:

C |Am |F |G |F |G |F |G ...

Another is to create the expectation that a chord sequence will resolve in a particular place, and then delay things by inserting an extra chord or chords. For example, the chord sequence C major, G major, F major resolves naturally back to C major: that's where we automatically expect it to go next. We could delay the resolution by repeating the G and F chords, as described above, but we could also do so by moving from the F major to F minor before returning to C. In doing so, we add an extra layer of tension into the proceedings, so the delayed resolution stands out more (Green Day's 'Wake Me Up When September Ends' uses this trick). And, of course, you can use a longer chord sequence which doesn't resolve to the root chord until the end. There's no reason why pop songs have to be based on a repeated two-, four- or even eight-bar loop of chords.

More complex chord sequences can involve other tensions and resolutions in other places, not just when they return to the root chord, but for the time-being, let's focus on this one. It's something that can be very important when we're trying out chord sequences to fit under a hook, and it may well be the key to developing that hook into a complete song.

When we came up with our vocal hooks in Chapter 03, we were thinking mainly of two sorts of hook. One was something that could work as the first line of a song; the other was a phrase or sentence that would become, or could include, the title of a song. Let's think about how the two types might relate to the chord sequence. It often pays to link the point where the chord sequence resolves to the root chord with a parallel point in the lyrics. In other words, if your vocal hook is expressing something final, answering a question, closing a debate, having the last word, or summing up what went before, the moment where that happens often fits well with a resolution to the root chord.

You can find examples of this throughout pop music. Take, for instance, the Sex Pistols' 'Anarchy In The UK'. The chorus consists of a single hook line that sums up the sentiment of the verses: 'I wanna be… anarchy!'. Part of the reason it works as a hook is the way the final, stressed syllable of that line coincides with the return to the root chord. Everything is working together to tell us that that section of the song is over. For other examples, you could listen to Abba's 'Waterloo' ('Finally facing my *Wa*terloo'), Oasis's 'Don't Look Back In Anger' ('Don't look back in anger, at least not to*day*') or 'Golden Brown' by the Stranglers ('Never a frown / with golden *brown*').

Other vocal hooks might lead more naturally away from the root chord. For instance, a great first line is usually one that begins a story, introduces a character, or just makes you curious to hear the next line. Resolving to the root chord at the end of the first line could work against the job of the words, which would be to hook you in to listening to the rest of the song. Instead, you might prefer to postpone the sense of finality and ending that a resolution brings until later on. Perhaps, for instance, the song would start on the root chord, wander away from it and then return for the first bar of the chorus, before resolving again at the end of the chorus or the start of the next verse.

So let's return to our hypothetical vocal hook that uses the notes C, E, F, D, G, D and C. We've already seen that even within the key of C major there is more than one chord sequence that could go with it, and that some of these might be more natural than others in terms of how each chord follows from its predecessor. Now we can also see how we might want to use a different chord sequence depending on where this hook comes in the song.

If that hook is the last line of the chorus, and we want it to sound final, we should use a chord sequence that resolves to C major on the last note, such as:

Am |Dm |G |C

However, if it's the first line, we might deliberately choose a sequence that doesn't resolve to C major, like this:

C |Dm |G |F

Or this:

C |Dm |G |Am

Both of these sequences will fit all the notes in our hook, and because neither resolves to C major at the end, they leave open lots of directions for the next line to take. If we wanted to take that idea to extremes, we could even use a chord sequence such as this:

C |B♭ |Gm |Cm

In this case, by heading consistently in one direction around our circular chord diagram, we've ended up quite a long way away from the root chord of C major; and if the song is going to return there, we've committed ourselves to a few more chord changes before that resolution can easily happen. In all three, we've left ourselves in a position where the vocal hook and its accompanying chord sequence are incomplete: we've set them up to be part of a greater whole, but we don't yet know what the rest of that whole will be like. Instead of choosing to drive round in a circle and come back to the place we started from, we've deliberately got ourselves lost. Getting back again might be an adventure, but ultimately, it'll be more rewarding.

Building from a hook

Assuming we're starting from a position where we have a vocal hook and the beginning of a chord sequence, the obvious question is 'Where next?'. Even if they don't rely on an obvious cycle of three or four chords, almost all songs are built out of one or more repeating sections. Depending on their role within the song, we call these sections verses, choruses, bridges, middle eights and so on, and in Chapter 07 we'll be looking at how the overall structure of a song is constructed from these elements. For the time-being, however, let's stick to thinking about how we might put together a single section in such a way as to make it satisfying.

What could make a collection of vocal lines and chords seem like a complete section with a natural start and end point, rather than just a random assemblage? One answer that we've already considered is that the chord sequence might resolve to the root chord at the end. Another is that the words, taken together, form a natural whole, as they do in a chapter of a novel. A third is that the melody as a whole might have a pleasing symmetry or shape that suggests development towards a conclusion.

When you become more practised at writing songs, you'll find yourself almost unconsciously taking all these considerations and more into account as you work. Developing a hook involves extending the melody, the lyrics and the chord sequence, and progress can be achieved by thinking about any one of these aspects, or all three simultaneously. It's like fighting a battle on three fronts at once.

If you can't think what to say in the lyric, try working out possible melodies without any words, then think about exactly what patterns of syllables fit them. Alternatively, use nonsense words, or repeat the words of your hook over again as a temporary measure. If you can't think of a natural melody for the line that follows your hook, experiment by taking the chords in different directions. Different chord sequences will certainly suggest different directions, and it can also be helpful to think about the overall shape of a verse or chorus; imagine yourself 'zooming out' from it so as to see only the broad outline of the melody. What sort of shape should it have? Try taking the same distant view of other people's songs to see what works and what doesn't.

On a more detailed level, there are ways to develop a single line into a longer section without just repeating it unchanged. Perhaps the second line could have the same sort of shape as the first line, but starting from a different place. You could try reversing the melody of the first line and using that for the second, or rearranging it by dividing it into two or three sections and swapping them around. Another useful idea is to repeat the last few notes of the first line as the beginning of the next line; the same sequence of three or four notes might suggest a new continuation when you move it to this different context.

Perhaps the most important factor in developing a melody is the lyric. Think of a memorable lyric, and the chances are that a catchy tune will follow: the way you go about developing your song's lyrics can kick the melodic part of your brain into action too. In the next chapter, then, we'll be looking in more detail at lyrics.

Listen to tracks 9 and 10 on the CD.

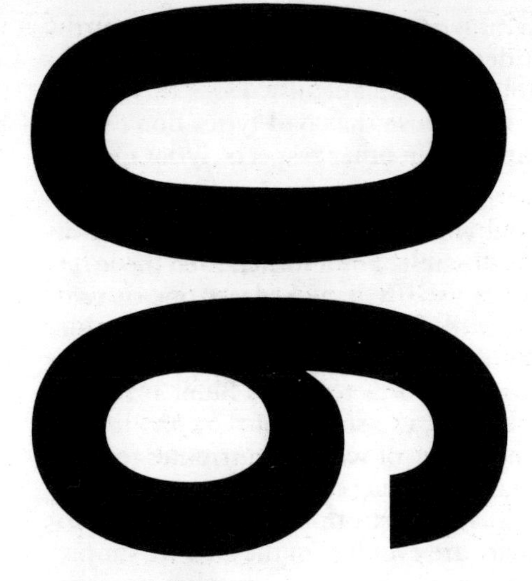

06 developing lyrics

In this chapter you will learn:

- **why lyrics matter**
- **why and how to establish a voice for your song**
- **what the different types of rhyme are, and how to use them**
- **how to use metaphor and other figures of speech**
- **how to make your lyrics more memorable and truthful.**

Lots of pop songs have awful lyrics. We can all think of records that have been huge hits despite having words that are dull, contrived, incomprehensible or just plain silly. Does this mean that lyrics don't matter? In the sense that bad lyrics don't stop records from selling, perhaps. But in other respects, lyrics matter very much indeed.

For one thing, any songwriter who takes pride in his or her work will want it to be as good as possible. For another, even those hit songs that have terrible lyrics usually have at least one or two vocal lines that stick in the mind. The lyrics would be laughable if written down in the form of a poem, but they allow the singer to create a memorable hook: the words to James Blunt's 'You're Beautiful' are prosaic at best, but the sound of that one line is somehow infectious, and the choice of words contributes to that quality. Bad lyrics are no barrier to success, but having nothing for a singer to work with is. It's worth thinking about why so few songs in foreign languages are ever hits in the UK: we simply tune out when we hear French or German, in a way that even the worst English lyric can't achieve.

Furthermore, in a world where ordinary lyrics are the norm, a lyric that stands out can make a big contribution to the success of a song and its writer. Would Jarvis Cocker or the Arctic Monkeys have achieved fame without their unique ways with words?

There's also a more subtle, but perhaps even more important sense in which lyrics are important to the process of writing songs. As we saw in our initial search for vocal hooks, the lyric doesn't just ride piggyback on the melody: it dominates the melody, constraining the ways it can move, bringing rhythms and shapes to mind. This is something that will come into sharper view when we look at rhyme, and in particular, the idea that songs don't have to consist of repeated lines that are all the same length. With a boring or repetitive lyric, we often struggle to generate anything other than a boring and repetitive melody. By contrast, a lyric with a less four-square structure suggests a whole new range of melodic possibilities.

What are lyrics for?

Let's take a moment to think about why we bother writing lyrics at all. After all, it's the part of songwriting that many people find most difficult, so why not skip it entirely and just sing 'la, la, la'? One crucial reason we've already explored, and will explore further, is that words help to guide us in the process of writing melodies. On top of that, most of us would probably agree that we want our songs to say something that can't be expressed by just using musical instruments, or by humming. A pop song can communicate to the listener in a lot of different ways, and can provoke a whole range of emotional reactions such as laughter, surprise, shock, joy, fear, disgust, sadness, anger or warmth. The lyrics are central to its ability to achieve this.

Sometimes, songwriters know at the outset what they want the song they're writing to do. You might have in mind a story that you want to tell, or a message you want to communicate to the world. You might want to lay into a former lover or seduce a new one. In that case, the process of writing the lyrics is a matter of finding the best way to express that sentiment or message. It's a question of putting flesh on the bones of an idea.

More often, in all probability, songwriters begin a song because they happen to hit upon a lyric fragment that strikes them as memorable: the sort of potential hook we looked for in Chapter 03 and developed in Chapter 05. A song begun in this way might not ever have a clear, central idea that could be summed up in one sentence, or the idea might come to mind only after you've gone some way down the path towards writing the song.

Even if you begin with a firm idea of what you want the song to do, though, the method suggested in this book is still applicable. Even if you begin with the best idea in the world, you still need to find a 'way in': a clue as to how to turn that idea into words that can be set to music. And if you can find a hook line that sums up or expresses your idea, you'll have the perfect starting point for developing that idea into a complete song.

We've already looked at how you might go about coming up with vocal hooks, perhaps including the first line of a song or the line that contains its title. The plan was to use these hooks as the kernel around which the rest of the song can form, like a pearl around a grain of sand. So far, we've considered ways to create the sort of musical foundation for that hook that has the potential to be extended into a whole song or a section of a song, whether by simple repetition or through a more complex chord sequence. Now let's focus on the words themselves, and how they might be extended or developed to form a complete set of lyrics.

Guided by voices

There are various features of any piece of writing, including a set of lyrics, that apply both to the whole thing and to every individual line within it. This means that if you start from an individual hook line, you've already fixed certain things about the lyric as a whole. Perhaps the most important is the *voice* of the words. Every sentence in the English language has, or implies, a voice; and when we put together lots of sentences, their voices need to be consistent.

At its most basic level, establishing a voice is about deciding the relationship between the singer of the song and what he or she is singing about. All songs need to have a perspective, or a point of view. Is the singer describing his or her own feelings, or talking about things that have happened to him or her? Or is the singer a neutral observer, simply reporting on events?

The former is called writing 'in the first person'. A first-person lyric is one that is presented as though the singer is talking about him- or herself, or about events they were personally involved in. It uses the pronouns 'I' or 'we' to describe events. This is the most common way to write pop lyrics, and there are millions of possible examples. From the Beatles' catalogue alone you could point to 'Yesterday', 'I Feel Fine', 'I'm Down', and many more. In general, we would describe a song as being in the first person if any of its lines are in the first person, because it only takes a single use of 'I', 'me', 'we' or 'us' to establish the idea that the singer is personally involved in what's going on.

Another 'voice' known as the second person uses the pronoun 'you'. In the second person, the singer is addressing another person or group of people directly. It's common for some of the lines in a song to be delivered in the second person, but pretty rare for an entire song to be in the second person (one example that comes close is Bob Dylan's 'Like A Rolling Stone'; another is the Beatles' 'Hey Jude'). Writing in the second person implies that the singer is not a neutral observer, but someone who has an interest in what's going on, so it's often natural to combine first- and second-person lines.

When the singer's voice is detached from what the song is talking about, we're writing in what's called the third person, using only pronouns such as 'he', 'she', 'it' and 'they'. Lou Reed's 'Walk On The Wild Side' is a good example, as is 'Maxwell's Silver Hammer' by the Beatles. In both cases, the singer is simply describing things that are happening or that have happened, without suggesting that he or she is in any way involved in those events. Songs that tell a story often take this form, but as a rule, the third person is more often used for individual lines, or even whole sections of a song, rather than entire songs. Another Beatles song, 'Eleanor Rigby', uses the third person to tell a story in the verses, but switches to the second person in the choruses, addressing the listener directly, telling us to 'look at all the lonely people'.

We mentioned that consistency of voice is important in a song, as indeed it is in any sort of writing. This doesn't mean that every line in the song has to use the same voice; as we've seen, any song that's in the first person is likely to include numerous lines in the third and perhaps second person too. What it does mean is that we shouldn't use multiple voices to talk about the same thing unless we have a good reason to do so. For instance, if you begin addressing someone as 'you', it's just bewildering to later talk about that same person as 'she' or 'he'. Likewise, it can be confusing to slip between the first person singular ('I') and plural ('we') without good reason.

On the other hand, if you do have good reason, switching voices or points of view within a song can be highly effective. A good example is 'She's Leaving Home' by the Beatles. For the most part, it's in the third person, simply describing the actions of a girl walking out of her parents' house; both the girl and the parents are described using third-person pronouns like 'she' and 'he'. At the end, however, the song switches into the first person, adopting the perspective of the parents ('We gave her most of our lives…'). It's a brilliant way of suddenly bringing home the emotional force of the events that were described in a neutral, detached fashion.

'Common People' by Pulp does something similar. For most of the song, Jarvis Cocker is addressing us, the listener, telling us in the first person the story of his encounter with the girl who 'studied sculpture at St. Martin's College'. At the song's climax, though, he stops talking to us and starts talking directly to her, using the second person: 'You'll never live like common people…' Again, something that began as a dry description suddenly acquires a more personal dimension, allowing the song to pack a more powerful punch.

Listen to track 11 on the CD.

Voices and characters

In lyrics where there is a first person ('I') and/or a second person ('you'), it's important to think about who these people actually are. It might be natural for us to always write songs from our own personal point of view, using our own experiences as a guide: and, if we want to address them to someone else, to imagine that we're talking to whichever ex-lover or friend caused us to have those experiences in the first place. However, it doesn't have to be like that. We can use the second person to address anyone at all, or everyone at once; and the 'I' of the first person doesn't have to be the songwriter, or indeed any real person at all.

This is a key point, and getting to grips with it will open up new horizons for what we can do with our lyrics. It's also a good source of ideas for developing a hook into a longer lyric.

Take another look at the hook lines you came up with in Chapter 03. Some, perhaps, will have obvious significance in your own life, but they don't have to. After all, our goal there was just to think of some snappy phrases that would stick in the mind. If they don't seem to relate in a natural way to something that's important in your life, one way of developing them into fuller lyrics is to think about what would have to be true to make them important. In other words, we need to put ourselves in the position of someone to whom that hook line would be expressing something significant and true. We can try to do this in lots of ways. Think of a character in a film, book, TV show or play. Think of a common situation that other people find themselves in. Look at news stories and imagine yourself in the situation of the people involved.

Let's look at an example in some detail. Suppose we had decided that the phrase 'to the ends of the Earth' might make a good vocal hook line. As a songwriter, you could still employ that phrase even if you'd never been further than Basingstoke, by imagining different circumstances in which you, or someone else, might utter it. It could, for instance, be used by a soldier who's about to be deployed to a distant battlefield. That, in turn, might suggest ways in which it could be developed. Perhaps the soldier could compare his experiences with those of someone who travels the world through choice; or he could reflect on the family he's leaving at home. Alternatively, you could turn the idea around and have the song be written from the point of view of an anxious mother or wife. We could also think about who the song might be talking to. The soldier could simply be telling the story of his experiences with no particular audience in mind, but he could be addressing a real or fictional individual: his wife or children, his commanding officer, the prime minister, or the enemy soldier he's about to fight. He could even be talking directly to the listener as a real individual, emphasizing the contrast between his dangerous, alien circumstances and the cosy life of whoever is presumed to be hearing the song.

By putting ourselves in any one of these positions, we create a world that our song can inhabit. We limit the possibilities that are open to us, but in a constructive way: instead of having the paralysing freedom to say absolutely anything, we are forced to ask whether anything we say is true to the imaginary or real world into which we've placed our song.

Tenses

Tense is a way of expressing the relationship in time between the song and what it's talking about. Most songs use either the past or the present tense, or sometimes a combination of the two. In the past tense, things are described as though they've already happened; in the present, as though they were happening now. Some randomly chosen examples of songs in the past tense might include Lou Reed's 'Walk On The Wild Side', Johnny Cash's 'Ring Of Fire' and Prince's 'Raspberry Beret'. The present tense is more commonly used, and the innumerable examples could include the Beatles' 'Penny Lane' and 'Something', the Kinks' 'Waterloo Sunset' and 'Sunny Afternoon' or the Stranglers' 'Golden Brown'. Occasionally, songs also use the future tense, talking mostly about things that haven't happened yet: Buddy Holly's 'That'll Be The Day' and the Beach Boys' 'Wouldn't It Be Nice' fall into this category.

As with voices, multiple tenses are very often combined within one song, whether by a definite switch from past to present or a more general mixture of lines in different tenses. And as with voices, what matters is consistency. Obviously, there's no reason why one song shouldn't talk about some events that happened in the past as well as others that are happening now. What *is* a problem is when you switch tenses while talking about the same event.

Truth and songwriting

Some songwriters are reluctant to write their lyrics in character, or describe events that they haven't personally experienced, because they feel that it's necessary for songs to be true or authentic. However, it's possible to agree that songs should, in some way, be true, without limiting yourself to writing only in the first person and only about your personal experiences.

Truth, in and of itself, doesn't make a lyric good. You could describe your trip to the laundromat in painstaking detail, but whatever lengths you go to to capture the experience, it's likely that the result would be a crushingly dull song. So why do we feel it's important that our songs be true, and in what sense should they be true?

When we talk about truth and authenticity in songwriting, what we mean above all is that it should ring true for the listener. There is no point in writing about your own experiences, however accurately, unless you can present them in a way that strikes a chord with your audience. A songwriter with a good imagination might actually write a better and more truthful song about a particular experience than someone else, even if he or she has never had that experience. Likewise, a fictional character might be a better vehicle for the truth than a real person: Eleanor Rigby never existed, but her story perfectly sums up the sense of loneliness and alienation that Paul McCartney wanted to capture in the song.

Personal experiences are an invaluable source of raw material for songwriting, but in the end, there is more to songwriting than simply describing experiences. The best songwriters draw on their experiences to access a more general or higher truth; they create something that is true for all of us, not just for them.

Of course, we must all recognize limits to our imagination, and you do need to be very careful when writing about things of which you have no experience at all – especially if your listeners might have. You have nothing much to lose by imagining the experience of travelling to Mars, because no-one has a better idea about what that would be like. On the other hand, it would be astonishingly arrogant for a male songwriter to write about the experience of childbirth as though he had actually gone through it.

Meter and rhyme

Having started with one or more isolated fragments of lyric, we should now have some idea of the world in which they live. Hopefully, we have thought about who might be speaking, who that person might be addressing, what sort of circumstances they're in, and perhaps, what sort of general point the song should be making.

In other words, we've established in a general sense what the words to our song might mean. It's time to turn our attention to the nuts and bolts of how our song will say what it's going to say: the form of words we're going to use to express that meaning.

Most pop and rock songs use rhymes. However, rhyme is not linked to meaning, and nor is it any help in getting a meaning across. In fact, the opposite is true: the need to have songs rhyme can be a huge hindrance when it comes to saying what we want to say, because it severely restricts the choices of words we can make, and the ways they can be joined together.

However, the 'rhyme scheme' of a song is intimately connected with its musical properties, as was stated at the end of the previous chapter. Melody and rhythm work hand in hand with the lyrics in their capacity as sounds. As we've seen, the patterns within our hook line – short and long vowels, stressed and unstressed syllables – both suggest possibilities and limit our options when we're coming up with a tune. In a song or poem, those patterns are repeated or varied across different lines in different ways, suggesting more possibilities but also closing off more options. The connections between those patterns of sound are formed by *meter* and *rhyme*.

Meter

The concept of meter is basically just a more formal way of describing the pattern of stressed and unstressed syllables in the lines of a song or poem. This pattern can be broken down into smaller units called 'feet', which are often repeated. For instance, the first line of your song might consist of one stressed followed by two unstressed syllables, then another stressed syllable, two more unstressed syllables and so on. As we've seen, meter is related to rhythm, in the sense that when we sing a line, it's natural to make the stressed syllables fall on important divisions of the beat. Some meters work well with several different rhythms; others more or less force us to use one particular rhythm.

One of the features of most songs is that meter is shared across multiple lines. In the simplest case, every line in the song might have the same meter: that is, the same pattern of stressed and unstressed syllables throughout. (Note that you can often sneak in extra unstressed syllables on some repetitions, or leave them out on others, without disrupting the overall effect.) If that meter is of the kind that only really works with one rhythm, you'd then end up with all your lines being the same length and feeling the same when sung, and likely enough there wouldn't be much variety in the melody between lines, either.

Another very common way of writing lyrics is to have the meter repeat on alternate lines, so that the first and third lines share the same pattern of stresses, and the second and fourth lines share a different pattern.

At the other extreme, an entire verse or chorus might be made up of a single line, or of multiple lines that all have different meter. The song that used such a verse or chorus would tend to have a much less repetitive melody, but would it still feel like a song? If the pattern of stressed and unstressed syllables seemed purely random and unconnected to the rhythm of the song, no; but meter can be varied without being random or unmusical. One of the most common faults in songwriting is to be too conservative in use of meter. There are times when sticking to a very basic repeated meter can produce a brilliant song, but the best and most individual songwriters vary their meter to good effect.

Paul McCartney is one master of this technique. Consider the first verse of 'Yesterday':

Yesterday
All my troubles seemed so far away
Now it looks as though they're here to stay
Oh I believe in yesterday

Here, we have three different meters in four lines. The first line simply consists of one stressed and two unstressed syllables. The second and third lines, which are much longer, share the same pattern, with stresses on the third, seventh and ninth syllables (in the third line these are 'looks', 'here' and 'stay'). The last line is different again, with stresses on every alternate syllable (including the 'day' of 'yesterday', which is not stressed in the first line). Yet it's not random: there's enough structure in the meter for us to hear the words as a pleasingly rhythmic pattern of sounds, without the use of endless repetition. 'Yesterday' is a classic example of a song we would describe as having a catchy tune, and it's this unusual meter that makes the tune possible. Paul McCartney has written many other songs that have similar variation between lines, such as 'Michelle' and 'Lady Madonna'. If you want to hear the idea taken to extremes, listen to Syd Barrett's solo album *The Madcap Laughs*.

When we're beginning a song by working with a single hook line, the obvious approach is to look for a second line that shares the same meter, or a similar one. But why not deliberately vary it, as works so well for McCartney? Try, for example, to come up with a following line that's twice, or half as long as the hook line. Take a look at the pattern of stressed and unstressed syllables in the hook line, and choose a different pattern for the next line. This will open up rhythmic and melodic possibilities you might never have considered.

Rhyme

Another interesting feature of 'Yesterday' is that the variation in meter between the lines is not reflected in the use of rhyme. All four lines in that first verse rhyme with each other. If they all shared the same meter and melody, the result would probably be banal, like a nursery rhyme. The unusual meter makes the rhymes sound fresh and surprising, where another arrangement of words wouldn't.

Rhyme is one of those things that we all think we know about, but in fact, too many songwriters don't exploit it as fully as they might. What most of us think of as rhyming is actually just one way of using a tool that has many other applications. As with variations in meter, using some of these other approaches to rhyme can help us become better, more individual and more complete songwriters.

Two syllables rhyme, in the fullest sense of the word, if they share the same vowel sound and the same closing consonant, but have a different opening consonant. Thus, 'way', 'day' and 'stay' are all examples of what's called 'perfect' rhymes. An imperfect rhyme, or assonance, is where two syllables share the same vowel sound, but have different opening and closing consonants, for instance, 'bat', 'cap' and 'stack'. Assonances are often used pretty much interchangeably with perfect rhymes in pop songwriting, especially where their closing consonants are similar in sound.

The opposite of assonance occurs when two syllables share the same or similar opening and closing consonants, but use different vowel sounds. This is called 'half rhyme' and is almost never used in pop songwriting. That's a shame, because it can be hugely effective. A rare example comes from the first two lines of the Sex Pistols' 'Anarchy In The UK':

*I am an anar**chist***
*I am an anti**christ***

The jarring clash between the short and long 'i' sounds is exactly the right effect for the song.

Another under-used concept that's related to rhyme is that of alliteration. Two syllables are alliterative if they share the same initial consonant sound, regardless of the vowel and closing consonant. Alliteration is a more subtle effect than rhyme, and usually works best when it's repeated lots of times in a short space. For instance, the main hook line in Joni Mitchell's 'Big Yellow Taxi' has almost every stressed syllable beginning with a 'p' sound:

*They **paved** **par**adise, **put** up a **park**ing lot*

In the context of a poem or a song, rhymes and other effects such as alliteration are usually between stressed syllables, though this isn't universally true. We're used to thinking of rhymes as happening right at the end of each line, but actually, it's more often the final stressed syllable in the line that's important. If that syllable is followed by one or more unstressed syllables which are the same across the lines, the rhyme is said to be feminine. The first two lines of Pulp's 'Common People' provide a good example of a feminine rhyme:

*She came from Greece, she had a thirst for **knowledge***
*She studied sculpture at St. Martin's **College***

In general, in fact, it's an excellent move to free ourselves from the idea that rhymes must happen at the end of a line, because so-called 'internal rhyme' is another under-used technique that can be very powerful in the right hands. It often goes hand in hand with variations in meter, and likewise helps us to generate interesting, unusual and non-repetitive melodies. Here's an example of internal rhyme from Bob Dylan:

*The pump don't work, cos the **vandals** stole the **handle***

Here's another from Syd Barrett's 'Terrapin':

*I really **love** you, yes I do*
*The star **above** you, crystal blue*

In this case, the internal rhyme that occurs between the middle of the two lines is much more important than the rhyme between 'do' and 'blue'. Indeed, internal rhyme can take the place of conventional rhyme entirely, as in the Dylan example; or, at the other end of the spectrum, it can serve as a subtle support to a main rhyme at the end of a line. A key point to bear in mind when you're experimenting with lines of different lengths is that a word at the end of one line can form an internal rhyme with a word in the middle of another line. Here's a simple example:

I ***love*** *you*
But I'm ***above*** *the things you do*

Here, we've brought together two lines with very different meters: one short, one longer, one containing just three syllables, all stressed, the other a repeating pattern of stressed and unstressed syllables. By making a rhyme between the most heavily stressed syllables in each line, we've made it clear that this isn't just a random assemblage of words, but something that has the form of a song. Better still, we've left open the possibility that the meter could develop still further. We could simply repeat the meter of these two lines, but we could also introduce a third meter, perhaps in order to achieve a rhyme with 'things', or 'do', or even both:

I ***love*** *you*
But I'm ***above*** *the* ***things*** *you* ***do***
They only ***bring*** *your weakness into* ***view***

The multiple rhymes bind the lines together very neatly, giving the whole thing a firm structure and suggesting a definite rhythm, yet there's no obvious repetition.

In the section on meter, we introduced the idea of deliberately experimenting with lines of very different lengths. This will be doubly effective if you can use internal rhyme too. Think again about the pattern of stressed and unstressed syllables in your hook line, and pick out the most prominent stressed syllables that don't fall at the end of the line. Now think of a much shorter line that ends in a rhyme for one of those syllables. Or, alternatively, if your hook line is short, try to come up with a rhyme that falls half-way through the next line rather than at the end.

Listen to track 12 on the CD.

Five rhymes that have been used too much

Some rhyming pairs of words have just been done to death in pop music, to the point where they've become clichés. Here are some examples:

Crazy / Baby
Dance / Romance / Chance
Fire / Higher / Desire
Brain / Insane
Right / Tonight

Let the listener do the work

When you're working with complex meters and rhymes, it's quite often the case that you can come up with one verse or song section, but it's impossible to find another set of words that matches the same rhyme scheme for the next verse. If so, it needn't be a big problem. Once you've used a complex rhyme scheme once, the listener tends to 'fill in the gaps' in the other verses, even if they don't work as well. Listen to 'Maxwell's Silver Hammer' by the Beatles for a good example.

Rhyme schemes

We've already seen that most songs consist of one or more repeated sections, such as verses or choruses. Where a song has more than one verse, these usually have different words, but they fit the same tune, and thus have the same meter. Nearly always, they also have the same pattern of rhymes between the lines. The way that rhyme connects the lines of a verse or other song section is called its *rhyme scheme*. (Note that the concept of rhyme schemes doesn't cover internal rhymes or alliterations.)

Rhyme schemes can be written down using a very simple method where we give each line in the section a letter. The first line will always be A. If the second line rhymes with the first, it too is an A; if not, we label it B. Likewise, if the third line rhymes with the first or second, it's labelled A or B; if not, C, and so on.

The simplest possible rhyme scheme for a four-line verse is thus AAAA, which we saw put to good use in 'Yesterday'. More common four-line rhyme schemes are AABB, ABAB and ABCB (where only the second and fourth lines rhyme).

Elvis Presley's 'Jailhouse Rock' is one example of an AABB rhyme scheme:

The warden threw a party at the county jail
The prison band was there and they began to wail
The band was jumpin' and the joint began to swing
You should have heard those knocked out jailbirds sing

An example of an ABAB rhyme scheme, meanwhile, is this verse from the Beatles' 'Get Back':

Jojo was a man who thought he was a loner
But he knew it couldn't last
Jojo left his home in Tuscon, Arizona
For some California grass

Many songwriters tend to stick to the AABB, ABAB and ABCD rhyme schemes, but there's no reason not to explore more, especially if we're experimenting with different meters too. Other rhyme schemes that can be very effective include ABBA, AABCCB, ABCABC and so on. Try not just thinking in terms of pairs of lines, but of the song section as a whole.

Saying what we mean

If all has gone well, you should now be armed with some fresh ideas about how to develop your lyrics in such a way as to create richer and more interesting patterns of sound. These, in turn, should inspire you to come up with catchier, less repetitive and more individual melodies. However, we haven't yet touched on the other crucial aspect of lyric writing: what the words actually mean. As well as sounding right in the rhythmic and rhyming senses, the lines of a song need to *make sense*: the listener needs to be able to understand them as English words and phrases. Ideally, also, they need to fit together to make a coherent whole, whether telling a story or communicating a message or feeling.

The approach to songwriting outlined in this book begins with a fragment of a lyric and builds the rest of the song around it. If you work this way, you might not have a clear idea at the start of what you want the song as a whole to say. Some songwriters are content to let the overall meaning of a song remain mysterious, or to treat the entire song as a collection of fragments with no unified idea behind them. Most of us, however, like our lyrics to belong at least loosely to some sort of overarching theme or idea; and sometimes we want each line to follow very directly from its predecessor, such as when we're telling a story.

No book can tell you what to write about, but there are some pointers that might be borne in mind when you're choosing themes for your songs. We're often told to 'write about what you know', and a lot of people seem to believe that the only worthwhile function of a pop or rock song is to express their own inner feelings and emotions. Some people even argue that songwriting is a form of therapy. That's fine as long as you don't expect other people to listen to your songs, but most of us aren't content with writing songs purely to exorcise our inner demons: we want to perform them in public, to entertain other people. In that case, it's worth asking whether other people are really going to be so interested in our inner lives that they want to hear about nothing else. Your emotions and experiences are a crucial resource to draw on when writing songs, but the point is that you have to create something that other people can relate to.

Many other songwriters would say that imagination has as much to offer as memory, and that focusing only on your own experiences when writing songs is not only self-centred, but it means that you miss out on a huge range of other sources for ideas. Those who take this line will draw inspiration from anywhere: news stories, novels, films, paintings, conversations with their friends, things they see in the street, or whatever. That's great, but you do need to be aware of one or two pitfalls.

Writing about one's own feelings and experiences has been so prevalent in the history of pop music that the form of the pop song has evolved to suit it. By contrast, not all subjects are really appropriate grist to the songwriter's mill. Remember that a pop or rock song contains perhaps 100 or 200 words in total. In the right hands, that's plenty to dispense some pithy wisdom about love and loss. However, you may well find it isn't enough to say anything worth saying about the Arab-Israeli conflict, or famine in Africa, or the rise of Creationism, or the tangled story of your cousin who was going to marry this bloke but got cold feet and then decided she was a lesbian after all. Some topics are just so complex that it's hard to see how any pop song could do more than parrot glib clichés about them: you need to be especially careful with anything to do with politics or religion. If you're tempted that way, it's also important to bear in mind that pop and rock music is, at heart, a pretty frivolous and trivial thing, and that it would be incredibly tasteless to write a pop song about, say, the Holocaust.

You could sum up this warning by saying that pop music, on the whole, deals with small subjects better than large ones, and that where it deals with large subjects successfully, it's usually by taking an oblique angle or focusing on details. The Beatles song 'She's Leaving Home' is a good example. It is, in a sense, about a big subject, namely the way that parental love is fated to end in heartbreak when children find their own lovers and leave home; but it never discusses this idea in general terms, only through the specific story of the girl who is 'meeting a man from the motor trade'.

Metaphor

As we've just seen, the songwriter has a ludicrously small number of words to work with, compared to the novelist or playwright, yet he or she is still expected to be able to convey something fresh and arresting with these pitiful resources. It's crucial, then, that we learn to make the most of them, and the key skill here lies in being able to make words mean more than they say. The successful songwriter needs to be able to exploit the difference between the literal meaning of words, and their implication or associations.

Let's take the word 'crypt' as an example. If you look up its meaning in a dictionary, you'll find that a crypt is the basement of a church; but thanks to all the ghost stories and horror films we've seen, the word 'crypt' brings to mind all sorts of other things. Likewise, the word 'snake', literally speaking, refers to a certain family of reptiles. Ever since the Biblical story of Adam and Eve was written, however, it has also had associations with treachery, fear, deceit and so on.

One important way of meaning more than we say is thus to choose words for their associations as well as their literal meanings. If we wanted to describe a heartless person, we could say 'He's so cold', but equally, we could say 'He's a reptile'. This *implies* that we think the man is cold, since one of the defining characteristics of reptiles is that they're cold-blooded. However, it also suggests that other things are true of him: that he's slippery or untrustworthy, for example. In other words, the second sentence has more meanings than the first, despite having the same number of words.

Describing someone as a reptile is an example of a *metaphor*. Metaphor is one of several varieties of *figures of speech* which are vital to the songwriter. When we use a metaphor, we are saying something that is literally untrue. We're not actually suggesting that a human being could be a reptile: that would be biologically impossible. The point of saying 'He's a reptile' is to connect the associations of the *word* 'reptile' to the man in question. Our ordinary speech is full of metaphors that we often use without even noticing that they are not, literally speaking, true: 'The M1 was a car park this morning', 'I was on top of the world', 'She's got ants in her pants'.

A closely related concept is that of *simile*. We use a simile rather than a metaphor when we make an explicit comparison between two things by saying that one resembles the other, as in Nelly Furtado's 'I'm Like A Bird'.

Any form of creative writing, including songwriting, involves coming up with fresh and original metaphors and similes. 'You ain't nuthin' but a hound dog', Elvis Presley tells his rival in love, while Bruce Springsteen described his passionate feelings by saying 'I'm on fire' and Blondie sang about a 'Heart of glass'. A metaphor can be obvious, as in those cases, or it can be deliberately mysterious, as in Led Zeppelin's 'Stairway To Heaven', Oasis's 'Wonderwall' and Marc Bolan's 'Jeepster'. A metaphor can be used in passing; or, as in 'Hound Dog' or 'Stairway To Heaven', it can be the basis for an entire song.

Personification

There's a special kind of metaphor that describes an inanimate object as though it is a human being, and this can be quite a fertile source of ideas for songs. For instance, the Stranglers' 'Golden Brown' treats heroin as a person ('Through the ages, she's heading west'). By personifying an object, you can associate it with the qualities that people have; 'Golden Brown' compares the addictive power of heroin with the lure of the Sirens in Greek mythology.

Yet another way to develop a hook line into a more substantial lyric, then, is to think about whether it could be a metaphor, and if so, what for. Suppose, for instance, we started with the short line 'She changed the locks'. The most obvious way to develop that hook into a song might be to tell a story about coming home one day to find yourself thrown out of the family home; or, to take the other side, about a woman finally rejecting her feckless ex-lover, 'I Will Survive'-style. But there are also ways in which we could develop the line into a metaphor: 'She changed the locks on her heart', for example. Not only is this a more striking and unusual phrase in its own right, but it's also ripe for extension (it brings to mind other phrases: she threw away the keys, she barred the door, and so on).

If our hook line itself doesn't hold much promise as a metaphor, we can think instead about metaphors that might say the same, or related things. The idea of being locked out, for example, might lead you to think about prisons, or castles, or being lost in the wilderness.

 Listen to track 13 on the CD.

Get into the details

There's an old adage about the art of writing country and western songs which says something like 'detail is everything'. It's true, and it's true for every other musical style too. Introducing the right details into your lyrics helps to make them both more convincing and more individual. For instance, instead of saying 'She was dressed to kill', why not actually describe a detail of someone's clothing? By concentrating on the detail, you help to create the impression that you're describing real events that you actually witnessed, and you reduce the risk of using generic phrases and clichés. It's much easier for the listener to picture a scene if you give them one or two very specific images to build on.

How do we work out which details are the right ones, though? Well, ideally, they should be details that are significant, or unusual, or especially relevant to the story you want to tell; they should be details you can describe in a way that sounds good; and, most of all, they should be details that have associations that go beyond the bare facts. For example, supposing you want to mention a romantic meal. Just saying 'We had a romantic meal' is a wasted opportunity. Far better to focus on a detail of the place, or the time, or the food, or a minute event that happened at that meal: 'We had oysters and champagne', 'We took the table that was furthest from the light', 'She ordered for the both of us', 'We ate a little and talked a lot'. The detail alone is enough to suggest a romantic meal, but in each case, it brings other associations too.

When we take the idea of using detailed rather than general statements up another step, we find ourselves using another figure of speech that's perhaps even more important than metaphor but often overlooked: the *metonym*. Don't be put off if the word is unfamiliar, because the concept is very easy to grasp, and it's a hugely powerful tool for creating meanings that go beyond what you can baldly state in a song.

We use a metonym when we use a part of something to talk about the whole thing. For example, back when the air of London was choked by a million coal fires, people started referring to the city itself as the 'big smoke'. As with metaphor, our ordinary day-to-day speech is full of examples of metonyms that we usually don't even notice. We refer to our cars as motors or wheels, the cinema as the silver screen, the theatre as the stage, alcohol as the bottle, and so on.

Metonyms are a powerful way of using details to imply wider meanings, because, for example, the phrase 'big smoke' has its own associations, which the name 'London' does not; it also implies that we want to focus on a particular aspect of city life. Like metaphors, metonyms can be used in passing, or as the basis for an entire song. Neil Young's 'The Needle And The Damage Done', for instance, is another song about heroin, but it refers to the drug metonymically, talking specifically about the needle used to inject it. In general, though, metonyms are not as widely used in songwriting as metaphors, which is a shame.

Moving on

The aim of this chapter has been to give you the tools to develop a single line or phrase into a lengthier collection of lines, such as a verse or chorus, and eventually an entire song. We've explored ways to come up with an overarching theme or idea for a song by thinking about the possible meanings that our initial hooks might have, either by putting them in the voices of different characters and situations, or by thinking of them as metaphors. We've also looked in detail at how to generate an interesting meter for a whole song section, starting from a single line, and how we might use rhyme in conventional and unconventional ways. Hopefully, this in turn has sparked off more ideas for how the melody for that song section might develop.

In the next chapter we'll be looking at the overall structure of a song. What are the different elements that can be put together to make up a song, are they all necessary, and what's the best way to join them together?

song structure

In this chapter you will learn:
- **about the function of the different elements in a song**
- **which elements your song needs**
- **how to introduce variety and interest by varying song structure.**

We've already looked at ways you might develop a single hook line into a section of a song. Now it's time to look in more detail at how the different sections fit together to make a complete song, and indeed why we might want to have different sections in a song.

The two most fundamental elements in the structure of a song are the verse and the chorus. Most songs have both, and they usually occur several times within a song. Normally, the different verses in a song have different words, while the chorus very often repeats the same words every time it comes around. Typically, the two have different rhyme schemes, meters and tunes; they may even be in different keys or tempos. They also tend to have contrasting functions in the song. For instance, the verses of a song might be like chapters of a story, while its chorus sums up the moral of that story.

Songs can have other elements, too, including introductions, endings, bridges and middle eights, while some songs don't readily lend themselves to being thought of in terms of verses and choruses at all.

Another way to think about song structure is to use exactly the same system we used to describe rhyme schemes. We call the first section of the song A, whether it's a verse, a chorus, or something else. If the next section is the same as the first, we call that A too, otherwise B; and so on.

The simplest song structure possible is thus AAAA... You might think that this is too repetitive and boring to make for a good song, but there have been hits that have had this form. When it is used, it's usually to tell a story, and there are lots of country songs that take this form, including Jeanne C Riley's 'Harper Valley PTA' and Johnny Cash's 'A Boy Named Sue'. Bob Dylan also used it on numerous occasions. Almost by definition, a song that only uses one element can't have a chorus (unless it simply repeats its chorus over and over again with no variation), but where the point of the lyrics is to put across a narrative, any sort of chorus would just break up the flow or distract from the story.

When we introduce choruses into the pot, we can simply alternate them with the verses in an ABABAB-type structure, but often it helps to have a bit more variety. You can, for instance, put two verses in a row at the start (AABABAB), or repeat the chorus at the end (ABABABB), and of course there's no reason why you shouldn't begin with a chorus before the first verse. When we get onto songs that have more than two different sections, the possibilities are endless. Here are some more examples of common song structures:

ABABCB – A basic verse-chorus song with an additional middle section

ABCABCABC – A typical verse-bridge-chorus song

ABABABC – A verse-chorus song with an additional ending

ABCBCDBC – A verse-chorus song with an extra introduction (A) and middle section (D)

ABACAB – A verse-chorus song where the second chorus is replaced by an alternative middle section.

Exercise

Listen to some of your favourite songs and try to write down the song structure using the system we've outlined here. Are they all the same? Do songs in different styles tend to use different types of structure? Are every verse and chorus exactly the same, or are there slight variations?

How much variety do you need?

Does your song need to have a chorus, a bridge and so on? Sometimes choruses are made superfluous by the fact that the main vocal hook is repeated at the end of every verse. 'Yesterday' by the Beatles is once again a great example, as is 'Dedicated Follower Of Fashion' by the Kinks. In both songs, the verses are neatly self-contained, and the main hook line in the song forms a nice conclusion at the end of each verse; there's no need for them to do anything but go on to the next verse. In a way, that one line is serving the same function as a chorus: it's repeated at the end of every verse, it's catchy, and it sums up the point of the song. And if you look at the chord sequence that underlies the line '...he's a dedicated follower of fashion', you'll find that it resolves to the root chord in a pleasingly final way on the word 'fashion'.

However, most songs need a chorus, for one reason or another. Perhaps it would simply be boring to repeat the verse over and over again. Perhaps, in either a musical or a lyrical sense, the verse is not a self-contained thing, but has the feel of leading onto something else. Perhaps the main statement of the song can't be summed up in a single line at the start or end of the verse, but requires something more substantial. Or perhaps the chorus is the main event of the song, and everything else was written around it.

It's risky to make generalizations about the different properties that these sections have, and there are likely to be plenty of exceptions to any 'rules' we try to come up with. For instance, it's often the case that the chorus is musically busier or more dense than the verse, but this is by no means universally true (think of Abba's 'Mamma Mia', for example). Likewise, if you draw a map of the main vocal line through a song, you'll often find that the choruses tend to contain the highest notes, but again, it's not hard to find counter-examples.

In general terms, most songwriters feel it's important for the verses and choruses to present some sort of contrast, and there are many ways of achieving this. For instance, not only might the chord sequences be different, but they might move at different rates: perhaps each chord in the verse might last for two or even four bars, while the chorus changes chord on every bar. You'd expect the different sections to have different melodies, and this can be emphasized by adopting very different meters in the verse and chorus. And, as we'll see shortly, there are lots of arrangement tricks that can be used to make verses and choruses sound different, even if they use similar melodies and the same chords.

Another way of bringing home to the listener the contrast between verse and chorus is to put something inbetween them. A song section that serves as a transition from verse to chorus is usually known as a bridge, and as you'd expect, its function changes depending on the verse and chorus in question. For example, some songs have verses and choruses that are close to being identical: The New Radicals' 'You Get What You Give' is a good example. Here, the point of the bridge is to add variety, to prevent the song being an endless cycle round the same short chord sequence and repeated vocal lines. If it works, a bridge section in a song like this will manage to make the listener feel fresh anticipation and expectation for the chorus, even though it's not very different from what they've just heard in the verse.

In other songs, the verses and choruses are so different that a bridge is necessary to smooth the transition. For example, in some songs, both the verse and the chorus are self-contained musical sections, but they're in different keys, so placing them one after the other without a bridge sounds jarring. In this case, the main function of the bridge is harmonic, creating a chord progression that moves from one key to another. Other songs have a huge *dynamic* contrast between the verse and chorus, meaning (almost invariably) that the verse is very quiet and the chorus very loud. A sudden jump in volume sometimes works, but sometimes it's preferable to have things build up over a bridge. Yet other songs require a bridge to link the lyrics of the verse to those of the chorus, and many need bridges for all these reasons and more. And, of course, lots of songs include bridges for no better reason than that the songwriter thought of one and decided that it sounded good.

All of these things are true of middle eights, as well. These sections are so-called because, in the past, they would very often be eight bars long, but of course they don't have to be and often are not. The main function of a middle eight is to complement the verses and choruses by providing a contrast. Though it's relatively uncommon for verse and chorus to be in different keys, for instance, it's much more common to change key for the middle eight. Rhythms, melodies and arrangements also tend to vary, and there is very often a contrast in feel to the rest of the song, whether that means the middle eight being a quieter section in a busy, upbeat song or the opposite.

The idea of song structure is a useful one for analysing songs and finding out what makes them tick. It sometimes happens that you can be happy with every individual element of a song, yet aware that the song as a whole doesn't quite work for some indefinable reason. In these cases, a close look at the structure will often pay dividends, and make you realize that you need to change the order of sections, remove something or add something else to make it flow more naturally or achieve a more rounded whole.

On the other hand, it's a mistake to take song structure as a prescription or recipe when you're actually writing a song. If you have in the back of your mind that your song must have a middle eight, because most songs do, you'll be including one for the wrong reasons. Just as an unusual melody or rhythm can make a song stand out, so too can leaving the beaten track in terms of song structure. Memorable hits with unconventional song structures in recent years have included Franz Ferdinand's 'Take Me Out' and Girls Aloud's 'Biology'; looking futher back, you could think of the Beatles' 'Hey Jude' or Derek & The Dominos' 'Layla'. Sometimes unusual structures are created by forcibly welding two different songs together: it does happen that you find yourself with two half-finished, and apparently unfinishable songs that just seem to fit.

Another opportunity that can be missed if you pay too much attention to the way your songs 'should' be structured is that of varying each song section itself. If you think of your songs just in terms of As and Bs and Cs, you can fail to spot ways in which these individual elements might change and develop as the song goes on. For example, one device that can be very effective if you have a 'big' chorus is to not unveil it in full the first time the listener hears it. You might use just the first half of the chorus after the first verse, and save the full Monty for the second. You could even have a chorus that grows each time it's heard. You might choose to space out the lines in one verse with short instrumental gaps, and close them up in subsequent verses. You could have two verses following one another, but in different keys.

Listen to track 14 on the CD.

At this point, we have covered most of the elements that are traditionally thought of as central to songwriting: melody, lyrics, harmony and now song structure. However, songwriting is about more than writing down a list of words and chords for someone else to play. It's about creating something that actually sounds good, whether that's a slick arrangement or a polished live performance. In the next chapter, therefore, we'll be looking at ways to take your words and chords and turn them into a finished recording that people will want to listen to.

arranging and recording your songs

In this chapter you will learn:

- **what we mean by an arrangement**
- **what equipment you need to create your own backing tracks**
- **how to fake other instrument sounds using MIDI**
- **how to record your guitars and singing, and make them sound good**
- **how to use effects and processing to make a polished recording.**

Musicians traditionally think of a song and its arrangement as two separate things. After all, the same song can be arranged for a jazz big band, a punk group, solo acoustic guitar or a minimalist techno outfit. Lots of Beatles songs have been arranged for all of the above and more. But if we look closely, the boundary between song and arrangement is usually blurred, especially in modern music. As we saw earlier, it is hooks that make a song into a hit, and those hooks aren't always the sort of thing you can capture by writing down notes and chords. These days, it's often the case that most of the hooks in a record come about because the producer has chosen interesting sounds on a synthesizer, or blended samples from other people's records in a fresh way. Is the horn sample in Beyonce's 'Crazy In Love' part of the song, or of the arrangement? Rihanna's 'SOS (Rescue Me)' is based on a sample from Soft Cell's version of 'Tainted Love': you could use the same notes without using the sample, but it wouldn't have the same effect.

What is for sure is that almost all songs these days *have* an arrangement, at least when anyone records them. It's incredibly rare outside of purist folk and jazz circles to hear an entire album of songs performed with nothing but an acoustic guitar or piano to accompany the voice. Even if you listen to records by acts we normally think of as being 'acoustic', like David Gray, KT Tunstall or Damien Rice, you're often hearing numerous human musicians as well as synths and samplers playing 'programmed' rhythms. And songwriters are as likely to begin with part of the arrangement as they are with a vocal hook, often taking their initial inspiration from a sampled loop or a drum pattern.

This means that if you want to sell your music, either to a record company or directly to the public, you'll be expected to put flesh on the bones of your songs. The days when you could walk into the offices of a record company or music publisher and hammer out your latest composition on the piano, in the hope that it would be recognized as a sure-fire hit, are over – if they ever existed. Record companies are interested in selling CDs, not songs, and to convince them that your songs have the potential to sell, you need to show how they can be fashioned into a saleable product. In many cases, that means making them sound like finished recordings, of a quality comparable to those that are actually being released; and at the very least, it means providing a pretty good sketch of how they could sound if they were professionally 'produced'.

That might sound like making an already challenging task even more difficult: not only does the songwriter need to be able to write a great song, but he or she also needs to have the skills and equipment to turn that song into a finished CD. It's no longer enough to be Burt Bacharach or Carole King: you have to be Phil Spector as well. Isn't that a bit daunting for the beginner? Perhaps, but don't panic, because what this development reflects is the fact that making a polished-sounding recording is getting easier all the time. The reason that everyone will expect you to be able to make good recordings of your songs is because it's now possible for almost anyone to do just that, with affordable equipment and the willingness to get to know it. What's more, as we've already mentioned, this equipment actually offers a new path into songwriting for people who don't play a traditional musical instrument.

What do I need to create an arrangement?

In Chapter 02, we introduced at least two kinds of equipment that can be used to create backing tracks for a song. One is the workstation keyboard; the other, a Mac or PC with suitable software and hardware. There is, of course, a third way, which is to use real musicians, and in the next chapter, we'll be looking at what to do if you want to get a band together and play live. For the time-being, let's concentrate on what you need to do to get an arrangement together without help from other people. Many of these ideas will also be worth bearing in mind when you work with other musicians, too.

When we discussed computer-based music programmes in Chapter 02, we focused on one particular approach to making music on computers which uses 'loops' of pre-recorded sound. These are generally short, repeated sections (hence the name) of music, either created specially for the purpose or taken from other records. Loops can contain almost anything: the sound of a single instrument such as a drum kit or piano, a band playing together, a string or brass section, sound effects, human voices and more. Software such as Sony's *Acid* or Ableton's *Live* allows these loops to be speeded up or slowed down, and moved up and down in pitch so that they can be fitted together to make a coherent whole. Some workstation keyboards will also let you work with loops in a similar fashion.

However, using loops isn't the only way to get music out of a computer or a keyboard, and if you do play a conventional musical instrument, it can be frustratingly restrictive to work with nothing but pre-recorded snippets of sound. Fortunately, both computers and modern workstation keyboards can record sound, and if you want to have the sound of eight singers and 15 guitarists on your song, you can play all the parts yourself, one by one. Recording sounds requires some more equipment, which we'll come to soon.

Before we look at the extra equipment you need to record your singing or guitar playing, though, we need to introduce something else that is often the key to creating good arrangements: the idea of MIDI. Standing for Musical Instrument Digital Interface, MIDI is the system by which synthesizers, computers and keyboards 'talk' to one another. MIDI is what makes it possible to have a 'controller keyboard'. Rather than making any sounds of its own, a controller keyboard generates instructions: play this note now, stop playing this note, and so on. These instructions can be sent to a synthesizer, which will turn them into sound; but they can also be recorded by a computer.

To understand the value of MIDI, you could think of the difference between handwriting and using a word processor. Recording sound onto a tape recorder is like writing by hand: once it's done, it's fixed. If you want to change a handwritten page, you're limited to crude methods such as chopping up the paper and sticking it back together. Recording MIDI from a keyboard is like typing on a computer keyboard. You hit an 'A' and the keyboard sends a message to the computer, which in turn puts the letter A on screen; but nothing in a word processor is fixed. You can move the cursor around and minutely edit every word. You can tell the computer to display what you've written in a different font, or at a different size. You can ask the computer to check your spelling or grammar. And you can come back to what you've written whenever you like and make more changes. Compared to handwritten pages, word-processor documents are infinitely more flexible. On the down side, though, whereas every handwritten page is unique, a word processor always has a limit to the number of different typefaces and layout styles it can offer; and the handwriting font on your computer never *quite* looks convincingly like real handwriting.

Computer software and workstation keyboards can both record MIDI information, and just as a word processor spares you the need to have beautiful copper-plate handwriting, so MIDI means that you don't need to be a brilliant musician to create drum tracks, bass lines, piano parts and so on. If you're recording MIDI messages rather than actual sound, you have complete freedom to edit those messages after they're recorded. You can even piece together a MIDI part note by note, if you want to. And, like sound loops, chunks of MIDI data can be chopped up, repeated, moved up or down in pitch, made faster or slower, and so on.

Another key point about MIDI is that it doesn't tie you down to the sound you started with. Suppose you record a piano part from your MIDI keyboard, but you wonder what it would sound like played on an organ or a harp. No problem. You can change one setting and have your piano part 'point' instead to any other sound that your computer or keyboard is capable of making. And, crucially, you can have as many MIDI parts and sounds playing at the same time as you want.

The flexibility of MIDI is what makes it so valuable to the songwriter. Just as you can use a word processor to make an early draft of a document, and experiment with different ways to develop it, so you can use MIDI to create an arrangement for your song that can grow and change as you write the song. If you decide to add an extra verse, or you think that the whole thing should be much faster, or you feel like adding a string section instead of the piano, a MIDI project is versatile enough to follow your ideas.

More equipment for recording and arranging

In order to work with MIDI, you need three things: something that can generate MIDI messages in the first place, something that can record and edit them, and something that can receive those messages and turn them into sound. If you have a workstation keyboard, you have all three in one: pressing the keys creates MIDI information, which can be recorded in a part of the keyboard known as the sequencer. MIDI messages from the sequencer then get sent to the part of the workstation that makes sounds.

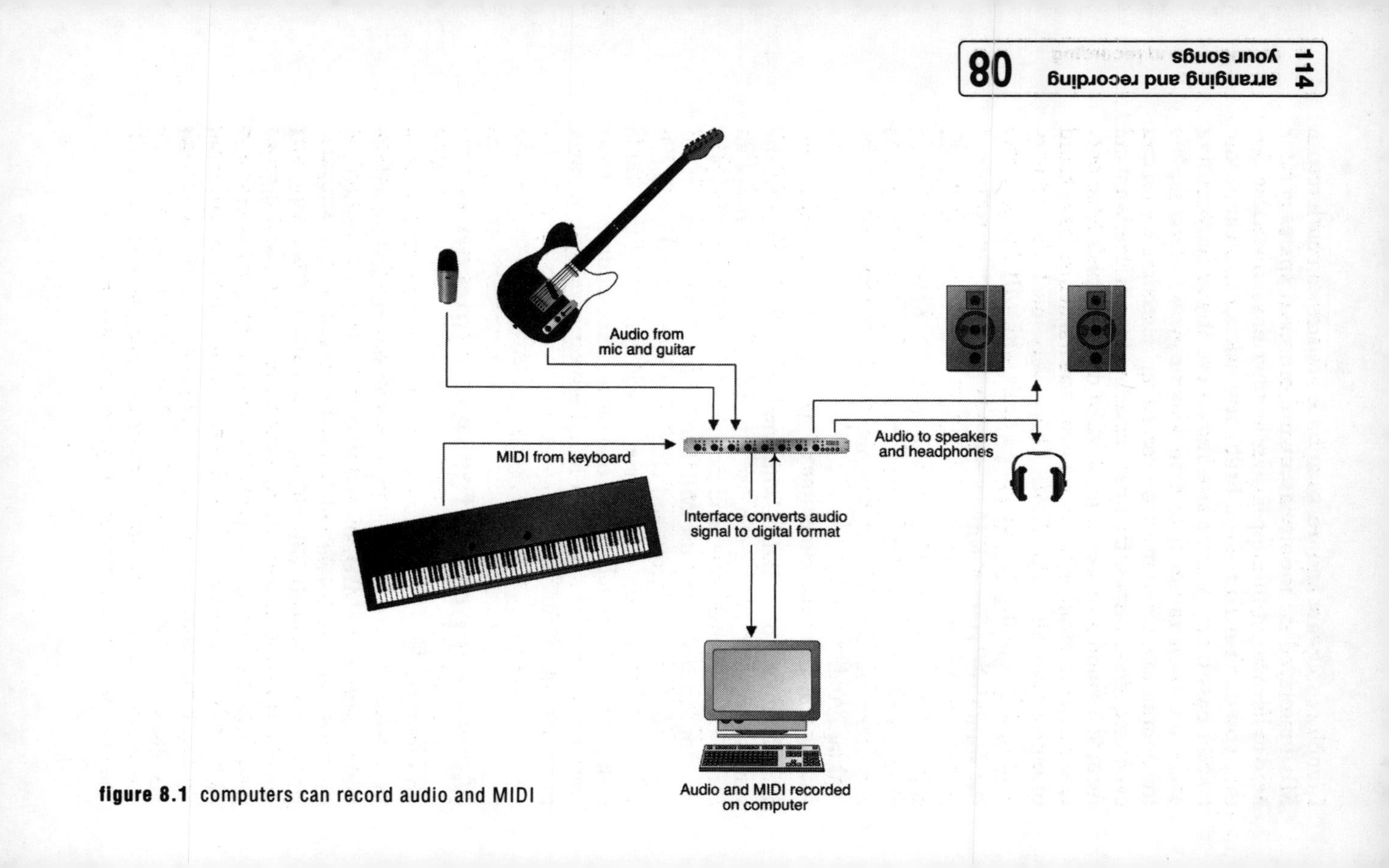

figure 8.1 computers can record audio and MIDI

If you're using a computer, things are a bit more complicated. First, you need some software that can record and play back MIDI information. Almost invariably these days, programs that can record sound also record MIDI, and vice versa. So, the loop-handling packages we introduced earlier can all handle MIDI and sound recording too, but there are also programs which are less focused on loops and more on recording. These are sometimes called sequencers and sometimes 'digital audio workstations' and include Steinberg's *Cubase* for Mac and PC, Apple's Mac-only *Logic* and Cakewalk's PC-only *Sonar*. You might also have heard of a program called *Pro Tools*. This is very much the industry standard for sound recording, and deals with MIDI too; it also works on both Mac and PC, but unlike the other programs, it requires that you buy additional computer hardware from the same company (Digidesign), which puts some people off. In general, the 'full' versions of these programs are all pretty expensive, but all are also available in much more affordable 'lite' versions that do everything you'll need.

Secondly, you'll need some way of getting MIDI messages into whatever software you buy. It is actually possible to do this from the ordinary computer keyboard and mouse, but this is a slow and painstaking process, so even if you aren't a keyboard player, it's worth getting a controller keyboard for this purpose. These are available in a huge range of sizes and shapes, not to mention prices. Whichever you choose, get one that can connect to the computer via its USB interface.

Thirdly, you'll need some way of turning those MIDI messages back into sound. With modern computers, the best way to do this is to buy more software. So-called 'software synthesizers' can make sounds that are every bit as good as the ones you get in keyboard workstations, and they integrate very tightly with the recording software described above. For song-arranging purposes, you'll want to get a software synthesizer that offers a good selection of 'real instrument' sounds such as drums, basses, guitars, pianos and orchestral instruments. Fortunately, most of the recording programmes mentioned above now come with free software synthesizers that will get you started. When you later decide to invest in something a bit better, some good options include IK Multimedia's *Sampletank*, Steinberg's *Hypersonic* and Cakewalk's *Dimension Pro*. There are also tons of software synthesizers available as free downloads on the Internet, though the quality can be pretty variable. Note that not all software synthesizers work with all the recording programmes, so you'll need to check that whatever you get is compatible.

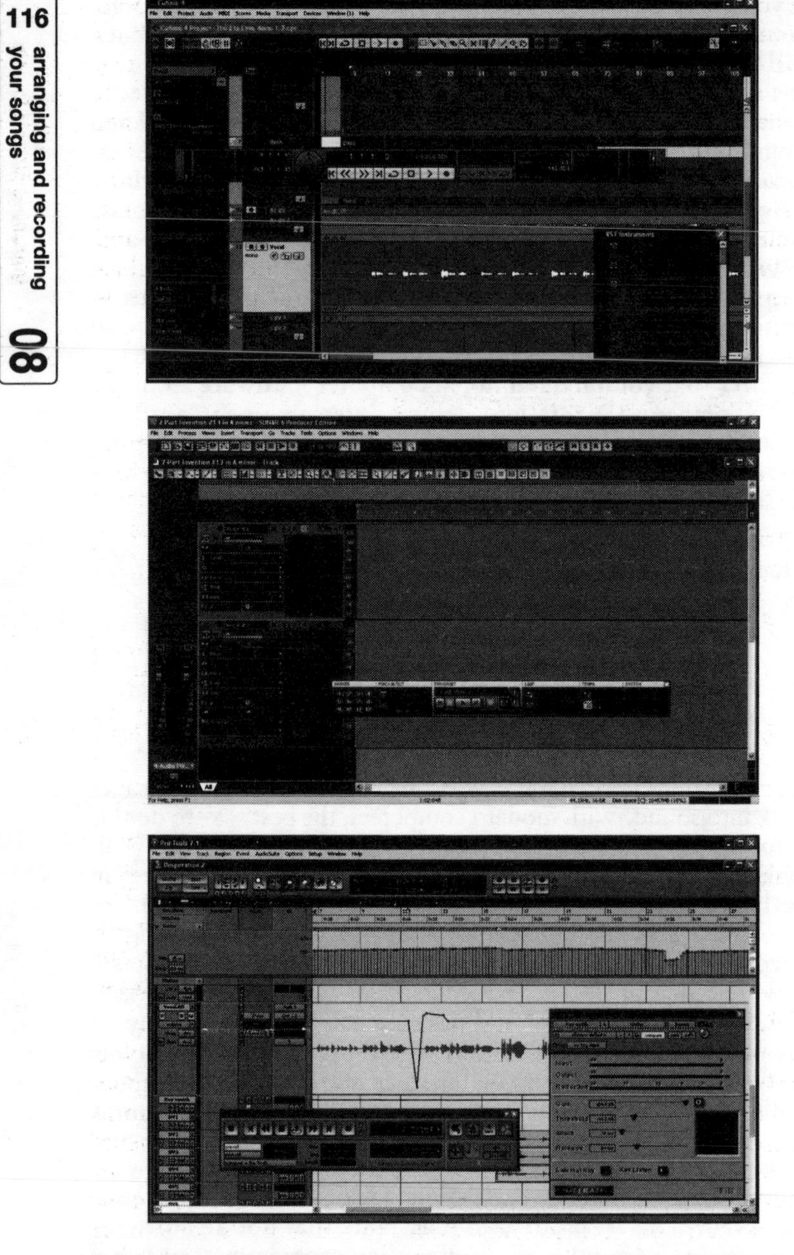

figure 8.2 popular programs for recording audio and MIDI include *Cubase* (top), *Sonar* (centre) and *Pro Tools* (bottom)

As mentioned above, *Pro Tools* requires that you buy an extra piece of hardware to attach to your computer. This is called an audio interface or soundcard and, in a nutshell, it provides a better way of getting sound in and out of the computer than whatever Dell or Apple saw fit to include as standard. The other programmes will work with your built-in sound facilities, but even so, it's always a good idea to get a proper audio interface designed for music. Not only will it sound better, but it should eliminate a really irritating problem called latency (see box) and will enable you to do more: for instance, some interfaces will let you record lots of different sounds at the same time, which is vital if you're recording an entire band.

Latency and computer recording

When you hook up a controller keyboard to your PC, you might find that there's a huge delay between you hitting a key and your PC producing any sort of sound. If so, you've run into one of the most common and most annoying problems with computer-based music: latency. The problem arises because home computers aren't really designed to be used as musical instruments in this way, so the built-in sound facilities are often not optimised for this purpose. You can sometimes improve things by downloading different driver software for your built-in sound hardware, but ultimately, the only satisfactory solution is likely to lie in buying a specialized sound interface designed for music. These are now available for well under £100.

The choice of sound interfaces available now is pretty overwhelming, and before you buy one, it really pays to do a little thinking about what features you are likely to need. For instance, you can buy models that connect to your computer via USB, Firewire or through the PCI slots in the computer itself, but it might be that your particular computer doesn't offer all these options, especially if it's a laptop.

Assuming you're not likely to want to record a full band, you probably won't need an audio interface with lots of extra inputs and outputs. What you will need is the ability to connect a good microphone so that you can record your singing and instruments such as the acoustic guitar. This means you should look for an interface with a microphone preamp that can supply 'phantom power' (all you need to know about this is that it's something that a lot of high-quality microphones need). Suitable models are available from numerous manufacturers including M-Audio,

Edirol, Terratec, Focusrite, ESI Pro, Presonus and more. Whatever you do, don't be tempted to buy a model that's designed primarily for games, rather than music. These often seem to offer lots of features for not much money, but can be a minefield of unnecessary complication and problems, including latency (see box). The basic rule to keep in mind is that if you can get it in PC World, it probably isn't what you want: instead, go to a specialist music retailer like Digital Village, Andertons or Sound Control.

And while you're in your local hi-tech music shop, you could think about getting a microphone too. Good microphones used to be ridiculously expensive, but the wonders of globalization mean that you can now get a really high-quality model for under £100. The main thing you're likely to want it for is recording your own voice, and for that purpose, a so-called 'condenser' mic is usually a good choice. The shop staff should be able to advise you on the details. Don't forget to buy a microphone stand and a suitable cable, as well; and don't forget that, as we saw in Chapter 02, you need some way of listening to your masterworks in high quality. A pair of headphones is essential if you plan to do any recording with a microphone.

Drum programming

Assuming you're tooled up with either a workstation keyboard or a computer and an appropriate array of add-ons, how do you use these to create an arrangement for your song? A good place to start would be to think about the typical ingredients you might find in hit songs in the same style, and a good ingredient to look at first is the drums. We saw in Chapter 04 that music is often divided into rhythm, melody and harmony, and that most instruments contribute to all three of these elements. In pop and rock music, however, there's always a fairly strong component that is rhythm and rhythm alone.

The rhythmic backbone of a song can come from lots of different sources. In a traditional rock group, it would be based around a drummer playing a drum kit consisting of bass or 'kick' drum, snare drum, hi-hat and other cymbals, and perhaps tom-toms and other elements. And although lots of modern records feature sampled or synthesized drum sounds, rather than actual recordings of a human being behind a drum kit, those artificial sounds often fall into similar roles. In particular, the basic beat is almost always marked out using something like a bass drum and something like a snare drum. Listen to music in almost any style, except jazz or reggae, and you'll hear the bass drum being used on the first and third beats of a bar, and the snare drum on the second and fourth. Often, additional, off-beat bass drum hits are used to create more interesting beats. More complex or busy patterns on hi-hats, tom-toms, cymbals and the like are added over the top to create a fuller rhythm, and there are often extra musicians playing tambourines and other percussion instruments too.

You don't have to start with the drums when you're putting an arrangement together, but there are several factors that make them the obvious choice. The first is that the drums are almost invariably the most repetitive element of the arrangement. Rock and pop drum parts nearly always consist of a simple one- or two-bar beat repeated over and over again, with only occasional 'fills' to add variety, and cymbal crashes to emphasize important moments in the song, such as the beginning of the chorus. If you're lucky, there might be a different beat in the chorus or middle eight, but often, that just means switching the hi-hat part to another kind of cymbal instead. What this means is that once you've got a basic beat sorted out, you can easily create a backbone for your entire song by repeating it as many times as you need. (Like word processors, digital audio workstations and MIDI sequencers will let you select a small piece of material and copy it as many times as you like.)

The second advantage of starting with the drums is exactly that they are neutral when it comes to the melody and harmony of your song. You don't need to be absolutely certain how your chord sequences are going to pan out in order to know that a particular drum beat is right for your song, so deciding on a beat still leaves room to experiment with other elements of the song or arrangement.

The third advantage is that when it comes to recording your other parts, whether as MIDI or through a microphone, it's vital to have something rhythmic to guide you. Any music programme will give you a so-called 'click track' for this purpose, but a click track is just a basic sequence of ticking noises, and it's much easier to play things right if you are listening to something like the rhythm you will want your song to have in the end.

The fact that drum parts are repetitive and don't relate to the harmony of a song means that lots of people use pre-recorded loops as the basis of their drum tracks, even if they are intending to create the rest of the arrangement using MIDI or by recording real instruments. You can 'sample' these loops off records and CDs, if you can find recordings where there's a section of drumming with nothing else going on, but you can also buy 'sample libraries' of loops designed specially for the purpose. Sample libraries can be bought on CD, DVD or for download on the Internet, and there's a huge variety available. Usually, they're themed for a particular style of music.

There are lots of ways to personalise a drum loop and combine it with others so as to create something unique to your song. For instance, music software makes it easy to chop up loops into their individual beats and move these around, so you can completely change the rhythm. Or you can 'layer' an additional percussion loop over the top of your drum loop to give it a busier, denser feel. With a bit of messing about, it's sometimes possible to separate out different bits from several loops and combine them to make a new drum part. If you've ever used a DJ mixer, you'll probably be familiar with the idea of 'killing' different parts of a record. This involves using a tool called a filter to cut out, for instance, all of the bass frequencies in a part. In the case of a drum loop, this will wipe out the bass drum and leave you with just the snare and cymbals, so you can add a bass drum part from another loop. All music software includes filters and 'equalizers' which can be used for this task.

Getting a basic drum beat together using MIDI is also pretty simple. Most recording software has a special editor window designed for drums. This takes the form of a grid in which each of the different instruments in the kit – bass drum, snare, hi-hat, toms, crash and ride cymbals – has its own row. The vertical lines correspond to the beats and sub-beats in each bar, and you can click the mouse in the grid to create MIDI drum beats. For example, if you want to have a bass drum on the first beat of the bar, you'd hold the mouse over the point where the bass drum row meets the first vertical line and click to create a note.

The illustration shows some of the most common basic rock and pop drum beats, as they appear in the drum editing window in Steinberg's *Cubase*. Feel free to copy these and use them in your songs. It's pretty much impossible to copyright a drum pattern (but note that it's very much possible to copyright a *recording* of a drum pattern, which is why sampling from records and CDs can get you into legal hot water if you release the results as a record).

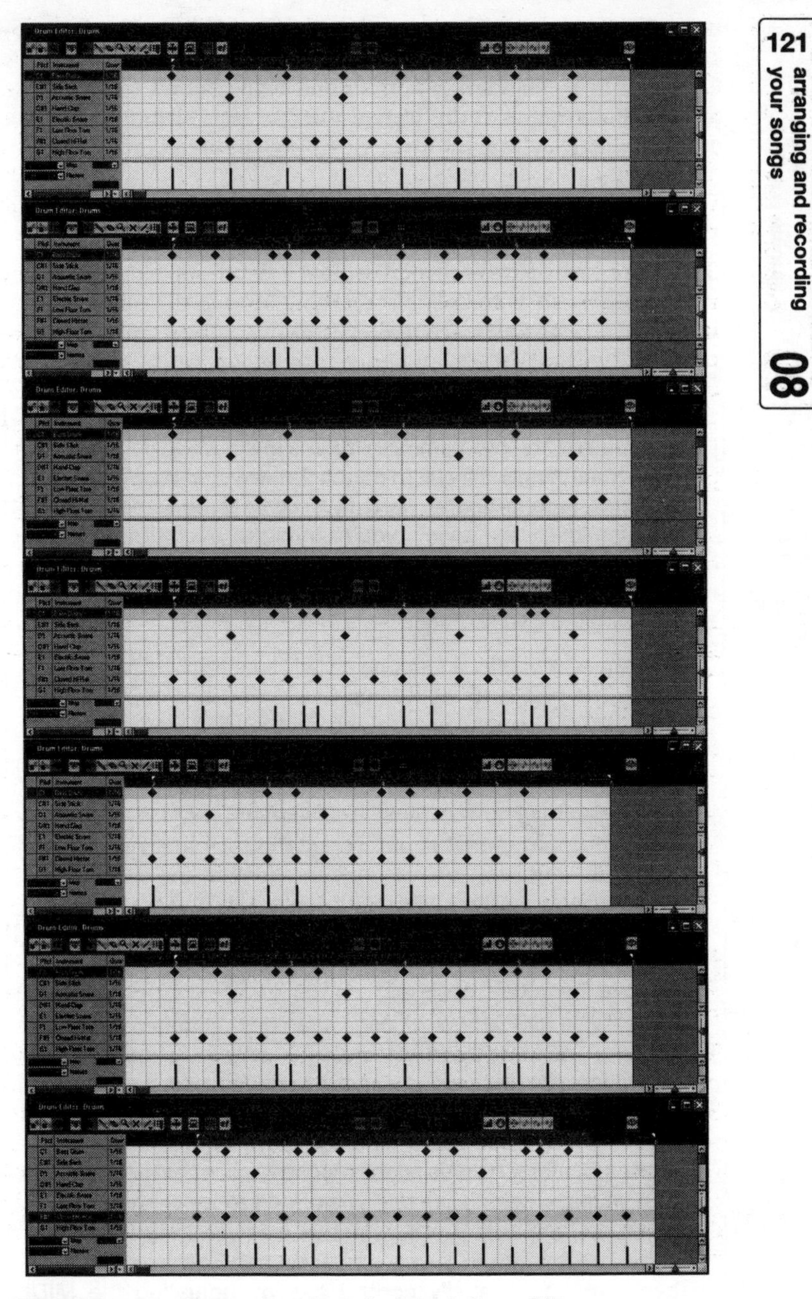

figure 8.3 some common drum beats in *Cubase*'s Drum Editor

If you're working with a computer, you could also look at so-called 'virtual drummer' programmes such as Steinberg's *Groove Agent*, Digidesign's *Strike* and FXpansion's *Guru*. These offer a really quick and effective way to get a drum part going quickly, and they're a lot more flexible than using loops.

Exercise

Listen to some of your favourite tracks and work out the basic drum beats. See if you can reproduce them in your sequencer.

Tips for better drum tracks

When you first try 'programming' drums using MIDI, you may find that it's frustratingly difficult to match the way that drum tracks on commercial records sound, even if you can get the same patterns. That's especially the case if you're trying to use MIDI drums to copy a real drummer. Don't worry: it takes practice, but if you're willing to put in the hours, it's possible to get very close. Here are some things to bear in mind:

- All sequencers offer a function called 'quantizing'. This has two uses. The first is to 'tighten up' the timing of sloppy playing. The other is to take a 'straight' rhythm and add 'swing' or 'groove'. Try experimenting with some of these settings: in particular, a small amount of 'swing' can improve the 'feel' of your drum track in an almost imperceptible way.
- Some modern digital audio workstations actually go further than this, and allow you to copy the 'feel' of the drum tracks from records you like. This isn't foolproof, and you'll need a good understanding of how your software works, but it can be worth a try. Look in the manual under 'groove quantizing', 'groove extraction' or similar.
- Typically, in rock and pop songs, the bass drum and snare hits are tightly quantized so that they play exactly on the beat, but the secondary elements of the kit such as hi-hats and cymbals, and other percussion instruments such as tambourines, often have a looser timing. You could try playing these elements from a keyboard, rather than using the mouse to click them into place.
- Likewise, the bass drum and snare tend to be very consistent in volume, while other rhythm instruments use some louder and some quieter hits to create emphasis and add interest to the beat. You can usually control this by adjusting the MIDI 'velocity' of each hit.

- An easy way to make drums sound fuller and more powerful is to 'layer' different sounds. To do this, copy your MIDI drum parts to another track, delete everything except the bass drum and snare hits from the copy, and use the copied parts to play a different set of sounds from the original parts.
- In a very quiet or gentle song, you might find that a full drum kit is too crude, and that percussion such as bongos, tablas and so on is all you need.

The basics of bass

The other ever-present ingredient in pop and rock tracks is some sort of bass instrument. In a live band, this would usually be an electric bass guitar, but there are plenty of songs that use bass lines played from a keyboard. The original Minimoog synthesizer, for instance, has provided bass lines to countless records. Pretty much any instrument can be made to sound 'bassy' if you play it far enough down the keyboard, but sounds that 'work' tend to have certain features. In particular, they usually have a prominent 'attack' at the start of each note, so that notes start suddenly, often with a kind of percussive 'click', rather than fading in slowly. Your workstation keyboard or software synthesizer will include lots of sounds intended for bass lines: some of these will be copies of a bass guitar, while others will be more synthetic.

A lot of guitarists play bass guitar, too, and the two instruments have a lot in common. However, don't expect to become an expert overnight. The right-hand technique in particular is very different and can take a lot of practice to get right. If you want to record a real bass, rather than play bass notes via MIDI from a keyboard, you'll need some way of getting the sound into your computer: see the section on guitars for details. However, whether you're using a real electric bass or an obviously synthetic sound, the role of the instrument is pretty much the same.

In a rock band, the drummer and bass player are usually known as the 'rhythm section', and the bass can be as important as the drums for establishing your song's rhythmic feel. Like the drum part, the bass often repeats the same short rhythm over and over again. Very often, most of the bass notes fall on the same beats as the bass drum hits, and this can be a useful starting point when you're working out how a bass line should go.

figure 8.4 the Fender Precision was the first mass-produced electric bass guitar, and is still one of the most popular

However, while drums are unpitched and thus not connected with the harmony or melody of your song, the bass line is the thing that underpins the whole chord sequence. So, not only does it have to have the right rhythm, but it has to fit around the chords. At the same time, a bass line can also be a catchy, melodic 'hook' in its own right. Sometimes the bass line can even be the most important instrumental part in the entire song, like in The Stranglers' 'Peaches', Deee-Lite's 'Groove Is In The Heart', The Jam's 'Town Called Malice', The Beatles' 'Taxman', Blur's 'Girls And Boys' and many more. At other times it fades into the background to the extent that you only really notice it when it isn't there.

Something that's true of almost all bass lines is that the bass only ever plays one note at a time. There's nothing to stop you playing chords with a bass guitar, or a bass sound on a keyboard, but they usually sound terrible. As a result, you don't need to be Rachmaninov to be able to play in your bass lines from a keyboard. Remember, though, that the rhythm of a bass part doesn't only depend on where the notes start, but on where they stop, too. Listen to the bass playing on records, and you'll often hear a gap between each note. These gaps can be as important to the overall rhythm as the notes themselves.

Because the bass has such a fundamental role in anchoring the chords of your song, and playing more than one note at once doesn't sound good, it's easy to fall into the trap of only ever playing the root notes of those chords. That's fine if you're in a punk band, but you'll need to be a bit more imaginative for pop and other styles of rock music. The ideal is to keep the sense of stability and 'rightness' you get from a boring root-note bass line, but add some interest by using other notes too. For example, as long as your bass line plays the root note on the first beat of the bar, it's already done the job of reinforcing the chord: you now have three other beats where you can play different notes or leave gaps. And you'll often find the note that turns your chord into its first inversion will work instead of the root note. For instance, if your chord sequence is C, G, F, G, you may well find that you can use a descending bass line with the notes C, B, A and G, thus creating inversions of the first G and the F chord.

Exercise

Listen to some bass lines in a variety of different styles of music, and think about what their function is. Are they just adding weight at the bottom of the song, or are they providing hooks in their own right? How does the rhythm of the bass part relate to the drums? Does the bass always play the root note of the chords?

Guitars

Electric and acoustic guitars are almost as ubiquitous as drums and bass guitars, to the extent that when a band without a guitarist (such as Keane) makes it big, it's headline news. However, their roles are much, much more varied. You've probably heard the terms 'rhythm' and 'lead' guitar, but in reality there's a complete spectrum of styles between basic strumming at one end and full-on axe-wrestling at the other.

Whereas playing sounds from a MIDI keyboard can be a very effective way of getting bass and drum parts together, it's pretty hopeless for guitars. You can sometimes get convincing results for electric guitar solos from a keyboard, but in the vast majority of cases, if you want guitars in your arrangement, you'll have to record them as audio, or use pre-recorded loops. If you're using a workstation keyboard rather than a computer, you may find this isn't possible, because some of them only do MIDI.

Assuming you have a keyboard or software that will record sound, though, there's a question over what is the best way to get the sound of your guitar into it.

There are two basic options. One is to use a microphone to record the sound your guitar makes. With an acoustic guitar, that means pointing the mic at the guitar itself: a good starting point is to point the microphone at the point where the guitar neck meets the body, from a distance of 18 inches (45 centimetres) or so. Don't point it directly at the guitar's soundhole, or you'll get a very 'boomy' sound. How good this sounds will depend a lot on the room you're recording in, so try different parts of your house until you find somewhere you like. With an electric guitar, you need to record the sound from the amplifier. You can put a microphone as close to the amplifier as you like, but experiment with the position, as this changes the recorded sound a lot.

The other option is to plug the guitar straight into your keyboard or your computer, which is possible with any guitar that has a pickup. This is called 'direct injection' or DIing for short. All electric guitars can be recorded this way, but by doing so, you're missing out the contribution that your amplifier would normally make to the sound. You can get special 'amp modelling' software to replicate the sound of the amplifier and effects pedals, and you'll probably need it if you want to DI your electric guitar. Some guitarists choose to work this way, though, because amp modelling software gives them more flexibility over the way their instrument sounds than a real amplifier. If you do plan to record DId electric guitar, it's a good idea to make sure that the computer audio interface you buy has a 'high impedance' input. Otherwise you may struggle to get it loud enough. DIing is very common with bass guitars, and unless you have a very good bass amp and microphone, it will tend to give better results with less hassle.

Acoustic guitars can be DId as long as they have a pickup in them, but when recorded through the pickup they tend to sound very brash and aggressive, and in fact not that much like an acoustic guitar! This effect is sometimes what you want, but can often be too harsh and unpleasant. However, there's nothing to stop you recording acoustic guitar through the pickup and a microphone at the same time. Then you can choose which you prefer later, or use a mixture of both.

If you originally wrote your song on the guitar, you'll have at least one guitar part more or less ready to go when you come to create an arrangement. The sort of guitar part that is based around strumming chords, or perhaps moving the plectrum across the strings to create arpeggios, is what's usually described as 'rhythm guitar'. Like a bass line, a rhythm guitar part contributes to the overall rhythmic feel of the song as well as laying down the chord sequence, and again, the gaps can be as important as the notes themselves. And as with a bass line, the role of rhythm guitar in a song can vary from being almost unnoticeable to forming the main instrumental hook.

Guitar styles and sounds are so varied that it's impossible to give any sort of prescription as to what you should play. Guitar parts for heavy metal songs have almost nothing in common with country or jazz styles, and in any case, your best guide is to listen to, and learn from, songs in the style you're writing in. There are lots of books and magazines with tablature for well-known songs, and plenty of useful sites on the Internet where guitarists can swap playing tips and advice on how to get specific guitar 'sounds'.

If you plan to use loops to create a realistic guitar track, you'll almost certainly need to buy a purpose-made sample library. You can certainly find sections of isolated guitar on records for sampling, but unless your song will be happy with just one or two chords, it's unlikely you'll have the flexibility to create a guitar part for the whole chord sequence. In fact, if you don't play guitar or know anyone else who can, your best option might be specialist software like Steinberg's *Virtual Guitarist* or Bornemark's *Real Guitar*, which are designed to make it easy to 'fake' guitar parts.

Better guitar recordings

- When you play the electric guitar through an amp, it can sound impressive just because of the sheer amount of noise you can make. That won't happen with the recorded part, however loud it was when you played it. What matters is the sound that you record, not the sound in the room.
- One of the most common mistakes in recording electric guitar is to use too much distortion. This doesn't make the results sound heavier or more aggressive, it just makes them mushy.

- One of the reasons why guitars on records often sound so 'solid' and substantial is that they are often 'double tracked'. This means that the same guitar part is recorded twice, on separate tracks, so you hear both in the finished song. With electric guitars, the player will often try to use different effects or amplifiers each time.
- You can make rhythm guitar parts sound fuller by using different chord 'shapes' when you double-track them. For instance, if your song is in the key of C, you could record one part without a capo and one with a capo at the third fret.
- Don't forget to tune the guitar regularly during a recording session.
- When you're using a capo, it's important to check the tuning of the guitar with the capo *on*.
- If you normally listen to yourself playing the guitar without wearing headphones, it can sound very different playing with headphones on, and you can find yourself playing differently as a result.

Keyboards

MIDI was designed with keyboards in mind, which is why it's so useful to have a keyboard when you're working with a computer, even if you aren't a very skilled player. No matter if you can barely play 'Chopsticks', you'll soon find that it's easier and faster to play drum parts and bass lines from a controller keyboard than to draw notes in software with the mouse. But what about the actual keyboard instruments that you hear on records: pianos, organs, electric pianos and so on? Can you get similar results without spending years having piano lessons?

Well, there's no easy way to make up complicated keyboard parts unless you can actually play them. If you knew what notes Elton John or Rick Wakeman would play over the top of your song, you could draw them in slowly and painstakingly, one at a time. However, the piano is such a versatile and complex instrument that the only way you can know what a 'real' pianist would play is to become one yourself. Compared to the guitar, it's much harder to use sample libraries to create realistic piano parts. Many guitar parts just consist of playing the chords to a rhythm, with minor variations, but a decent pianist will use the chord sequence as a basis to craft something much more involved; it's almost impossible to achieve the same effect simply by stringing together sampled loops.

All is not lost, though. For one thing, the wonders of MIDI mean that you only ever have to be able to play a keyboard part badly, because you can always move notes around afterwards to correct them. Once you've been playing keyboards for a little while, you may well find yourself thinking beyond your ability in terms of what notes your arrangement should use, and MIDI makes it possible to put these ideas into practice.

More importantly, although difficult or complex keyboard parts really need a keyboard player to come up with them, there are loads of keyboard parts on records that are actually dead simple. Remember that the majority of bands don't have an Elton John or Rick Wakeman, so if you hear keyboards on their records, that means that either they got a session player in to record them, or they were played by another musician. Very often it's the latter: the guitarist or singer noticed a Hammond organ in the back of the studio and decided to bash out something simple to lift the last chorus, or whatever.

One of the stumbling blocks that many people encounter when learning piano is that you are supposed to be able to play different things on your left and right hand at the same time. This sort of 'independence' is difficult to learn, but does your arrangement really need it? If the answer is yes, you could always record the left and right-hand parts separately. However, it's very often the case that only the right-hand part will be at all noticeable in the full arrangement. After all, the chances are that you'll have a separate bass instrument in the arrangement, so any more low notes you add on the piano may well be inaudible over the bass; and if they are audible, they might clutter things up and make that part of the arrangement too full.

Also, don't forget that keyboard instruments include synthesizers, and that synthesizers don't have to be used just to imitate real instruments. One of the great things about synthesizers is that you can create 'artificial' sounds which have lots of movement and interest in them, so that you don't really need to play anything very complicated. Often, you can just hold down a chord and the sound itself will evolve and develop in an ear-catching way. Any workstation keyboard will have a good selection of these sounds, and there are lots of specialized software synthesizers devoted to making them, including some excellent freeware and shareware programs you can download for nothing.

All in all, there are lots of easy ways you can use keyboards and keyboard sounds to embellish an arrangement, especially if they're a sideshow to other instruments such as guitars:

- Play each chord in the chord sequence, but 'arpeggiate' it – rather than playing all the notes at once, start at the bottom and work up.
- Some keyboard sounds, especially pianos, have quite a strong percussive element to them, so you can often add something to the arrangement just by hammering out a rhythm on one or two notes.
- Other sounds, such as organs, tend to be drawn-out, which makes them perfect for reinforcing a chord sequence in the background. Again, you can often get away with a simple part based around the chords.
- You sometimes find that your arrangement has a 'hole' in it which can be filled by a very basic keyboard part. For example, you can often add a very high-pitched keyboard sound over the top of everything else, because nothing else is inhabiting that part of the arrangement.
- If you have a melodic part played on another instrument, you can sometimes make it more interesting by 'doubling' it with the same part on a synthesizer or piano.
- Synthesizers are excellent for producing atmospheric sounds that aren't exactly musical, but help to create a mood for your song.

Other instruments

You'll notice that your keyboard workstation or software synthesizer can imitate a whole raft of other instruments, apart from the ones already mentioned. Some of these instruments, such as strings and brass, are often heard on rock and pop records; others, like bassoons or accordions, less so. Some lend themselves well to being imitated from a MIDI keyboard, while others present the same sort of obstacles as the guitar. Whether you can get away with using a particular sound from your keyboard often depends on its context within an arrangement. For instance, you might find that there are violin sounds that are OK if you use them as part of a string section in the background, but sound horribly cheesy and fake if you try to play an exposed violin solo.

Proper arranging for strings, brass or other orchestral instruments is something that takes a lot of skill and theoretical knowledge, but again, not all the strings and brass you hear on records are arranged 'properly', and it's often possible to come up with something simple yet effective. Very often, for instance, you hear strings doing little more than playing the chords, and as long as you leave them in the background, few people will complain (although this doesn't always add much to the arrangement). A typical keyboard string sound is long and drawn-out and can be used in a similar way to an organ sound. Brass instruments, by contrast, are punchy and loud, and demand to be used in more prominent roles: think of the brass sections on all those 1960s and 1970s soul records. It's quite difficult to achieve the same effect with keyboards, but there are lots of good sample libraries containing recordings of brass 'licks' by really good players, which can be perfect.

If you use a lot of 'real' instruments such as strings and brass in your arrangement, you need to take care over the balance between them. Stringed instruments such as violins and cellos tend to be quite quiet, for instance, whilst trumpets and saxophones are very loud, so you need to make sure that your arrangement reflects this.

Arranging advice

In arrangements, as with everything else to do with music, rules are made to be broken. But unless you have a good reason not to, it's usually a good idea to follow these ones:

- Every part of the arrangement should be there for a reason. This applies most of all to the beginning of the song. You're not going to impress anyone with a long introduction that just consists of you playing the chords on a guitar. Get to the hooks as soon as possible.
- Inexperienced arrangers often clutter things up by using a long, drawn-out sound such as a string section just to play the chords in the background. This rarely adds anything to the song. By all means use strings, but only if you can think of a string part that's interesting and worthwhile in its own right.
- If you're bursting with good ideas for an arrangement, don't use them all at once. Too many different things going on at once will sound like a mess.

- Remember that you don't need to use all your ideas all the way through your song. There's nothing wrong with having a guitar or a piano come in for half a verse, or just the middle eight, if that's what you want.
- Repeated sections of your song, such as verses and choruses, don't have to have the same arrangement every time they come around. For instance, a common trick is to 'drop' the third verse so that it's much quieter than the previous two.
- Trust your ears, not your eyes. There are lots of situations where things can look 'right' on your computer screen but sound wrong. For example, a drum beat and a synthesized violin note might look as though they're on the same beat, but the violin can sound 'late' because it's a sound that fades in slowly.
- When you're choosing sounds from a keyboard or a software synthesizer, the ones that sound most impressive on their own are not always the most suitable for a busy arrangement. There's only so much 'space' in an arrangement, and you'll often find that simpler bass sounds or keyboard sounds fit in better.
- Don't be afraid to change sounds. Almost all keyboards and synthesizers give you lots of ways to modify the sounds they make, and if you do, you'll have your own personal instruments to work with, not just the same ones that thousands of other people are using.
- Even if you aren't using loops to create your arrangement, you can add interest by throwing in other samples such as sound effects. Eminem and his producer Dr. Dre are masters of this technique: listen to the sound effects in 'Stan', for example.
- If you're unsure about your skills on keyboard, guitar or any other instrument, remember that there are tons of other musicians out there, and plenty of them will be happy to play on your recordings. Try using local Internet message boards, or put up notices in music shops.

Listen to track 15 on the CD.

Recording your vocals

The most important part of almost any arrangement isn't the drums, or the bass, or the guitars, or any squiddly noises on synthesizers. It's the sound of the human voice. An amazing performance from a singer can make the listener forgive all manner of problems with the other instruments; conversely, the most brilliant and imaginative instrumental arrangement can be let down by bad singing.

Up to now, we've assumed that you, as the writer of the song, will also be the singer. We'll be looking at the extra issues involved in writing for someone else in Chapter 10, but for now, let's think about how you can get your own vocals recorded as part of your arrangement. There are three basic things you need to get right. The first, and most important, is that you need to be able to give the best performance you can. The second is that you need to be able to capture that performance in your recording equipment. And the third is that you need to be able to fit the results into your arrangement as well as possible.

As with writing lyrics, lots of novice songwriters think of singing as something that should be as raw and natural as possible. If you believe that lyric writing is about exposing your emotions as directly and barely as you can, it makes sense to think of singing along similar lines. In both cases, however, most people come to realize that practice, learning and technique don't undermine their music. The more thought you put into writing your lyrics, the better you'll be able to express what you're feeling, and likewise, working at your singing will give you a more powerful tool for putting those words across to the audience.

If you genuinely want to become a successful singer/songwriter, find yourself a good singing teacher. This is not an admission that something's wrong with your voice: it's a statement that you are serious about your goal. However confident you are in your 'natural' singing voice, you will be amazed at how much improvement you notice after even a couple of lessons. You'll learn all sorts of useful things, such as how to warm up your voice properly before you go on stage. You'll learn good vocal technique, and if you're lucky enough to be offered lots of gigs, you'll need this to ensure that you're physically capable of singing night after night without losing your voice.

Singing lessons and practice will help you learn to perform your songs better in general, but there are also things you can do to ensure that you give the best performance you can when the 'red light is on' and you're recording your own vocals. That can be especially difficult if you're recording at home, and most people are understandably a bit self-conscious about belting it out in the front room. Getting it right is a bit of a black art – one of the reasons why top-name record producers can command huge fees is their ability to coax the best performances out of singers in the studio, but here are some things to remember:

- Make sure that you know the words and tune well, ideally off by heart.
- Take time to ensure that you're as comfortable as possible, not only with where you're standing or sitting, but with what you're hearing in your headphones. Some people like to hear lots of their own voice, others prefer to have it completely drowned out by the rest of the arrangement.
- Everyone's voice takes time to reach its peak during a recording session, but not everyone takes the same time. If you consistently find that you do your best performances early, say on the second or third time you attempt the song, there's no point in doing long sessions where you gradually get worse and more frustrated.
- Don't erase anything you record unless it was bad all the way through. You can record as many 'takes' as you like without needing to get rid of earlier ones.
- Keep a glass of water handy.
- Listening to yourself in headphones is very weird if you're used to singing without them. If you find it hard to get used to, try just wearing one of the earpieces, so you're hearing the backing track in the earpiece and your voice in the normal way through the other ear.
- Remember that you don't have to record the whole vocal part in one go. If there's one section that's particularly difficult, you can try just doing that bit over and over again until you get it right.

If you've created your arrangement on a workstation keyboard that will only record MIDI, not actual sound, you'll need to invest in a separate sound-recording device in order to capture your voice. You could either use a Mac or PC equipped with the software we've already looked at, or you could buy one of the many specialist multitrack recorders on the market from companies such as Yamaha, Roland, Zoom, Akai, Korg and Boss. These are dedicated hardware units that offer the same functions as recording software. They tend to be more limited than computer-based systems, but many people find them easier to use.

If you've got some sort of recording setup in place, recording your voice should be fairly straightforward, as long as you follow some basic principles and use your ears to judge the results. We saw earlier that a good microphone is essential, and there are now numerous affordable 'condenser' mics which will do the job very well, from companies such as Rode, Red5, Studio Projects, MXL, AKG, Sennheiser, Audio-Technica, Charter Oak,

figure 8.5 many people find dedicated recording machines, such as the Yamaha (top), Boss (centre) and Korg (bottom) models shown here, easier to get to grips with than computers

SE Electronics and many more. All of these companies make a range of condenser mics with different features: for vocals, a good starting point is a 'large-diaphragm' model with a 'cardioid' pickup pattern. Again, a good music shop should be able to advise you. All of these mics require something called 'phantom power' to operate. Many specialist computer soundcards will supply this, and allow you to connect a condenser mic directly. If yours doesn't, you will need to add a separate 'pre-amplifier'.

If you're recording in a room in your house, the ideal is to get the sound directly to the microphone from your mouth, and to capture as little as possible of the 'reflected' sound bouncing off the walls of the room. This means getting fairly close to the microphone (about six inches/15 centimetres away is a good starting point) and trying to minimize reflections, for instance by hanging a duvet behind the microphone. You also need to minimize the amount of other noise getting into your recordings: problems can arise from traffic outside your window, washing machines and fridges, and especially from hums and buzzes made by your computer itself.

The third aspect of getting a good-sounding vocal into your arrangement is what you do to it after you've recorded it. A great singer will sound great regardless of what you do at this point, but sensitive editing and processing can improve even the best performances, and will do wonders for less confident singers.

When you hear apparently amazing vocal performances on records from the last couple of decades, the chances are that the singer didn't nail that performance in one go. Instead, the producer and engineer have stitched together the best bits from lots of different 'takes', in much the same way that a film director will shoot each scene lots of times before editing the best takes of each into a sequence. This technique is often called 'vocal comping', and the manual for your recording hardware or software should explain how to do it. Failing that, there are lots of resources on the Internet that will help. Either way, once you get the hang of it it's not difficult, though it can be quite tedious. But it's definitely worth doing unless you're confident that one take was head and shoulders above the rest – and even the best performances often contain the odd dodgy word or line that would be better replaced.

Pop goes the microphone

Many singers find that when they make loud 'p' and 'b' sounds, the recording picks up a loud 'pop' that shouldn't be there. If you do, you need to use a so-called 'pop shield'. These are easily made by stretching a thin pair of tights over a coathanger bent into a circle. Put the pop shield inbetween your mouth and the microphone.

figure 8.6 you can buy pop shields, such as this AKG model, but it's also easy to make your own

A related idea that you hear on lots of records, especially on rap vocals, is 'double tracking'. As the name suggests, what this means is that you use not one but two lead vocal tracks at the same time. Sometimes this can make the lead vocal more powerful and forceful, but it will only work if you can sing the lines in exactly the same way each time, which takes a fair amount of skill. Some singers routinely 'double track' all their vocals, but it's often more effective to use the technique just for a couple of lines where you want to create an emphasis.

Another technique that's widely, if not universally used in professional music production is automated pitch correction. This, as the name suggests, is a way of putting singing in tune if it was out of tune. To do it, you'll need specialist tools (the industry standard is Antares' *Auto-Tune*, but Celemony's *Melodyne* is sometimes preferred), some expertise and a lot of self-restraint: it's very easy to ruin a good performance by trying to make it 'too perfect'. What's more, a bad performance will still be a bad performance even if you do put all the notes in tune. Too often, people see this technique as a get-out that will enable them to get away with substandard singing. If you're recording in your own house on your own time, it's far better to just do it again and again until you get it right.

If you want your vocals to sound at all like singing on records, though, there are two other processes you do need to investigate. One is 'compression' and the other is 'reverb'. Compression 'flattens out' the sound of your voice, making the loud bits quieter or the quiet bits louder, whichever way you want to look at it. The manual for your recording hardware or software will explain how to apply compression to something.

Vocals are usually recorded in a fairly 'dead' space, which is what you're achieving by hanging duvets behind the microphone and so on. The reason for doing this is that our hearing is very good at noticing the reflections that come back off the walls and guessing what sort of room the recording was made in. Some rooms sound 'better' than others, and most rooms in an ordinary house don't sound very good. By damping the reflections within the room, we leave open the option to replace those reflections later on with ones we've generated artificially. In other words, we can simulate the effect of recording in a whole range of different rooms, and choose which one we like the best.

This effect is usually called 'reverberation', or 'reverb' for short. Again, you'll find no shortage of information on how to use it in the manual for your recording equipment, and on the Internet. It's worth trying out a lot of different settings on your vocals to see which of them suits you best. You will also find that different settings work better on different songs: in general, for slow ballads you may want your voice to sound like it was recorded in a large hall, while more upbeat songs need a less expansive sound. Both compression and reverb can be applied in different amounts, and in both cases, you need to be really careful not to overdo it.

Backing vocals and harmonies

The lead vocal is the most important element of almost every arrangement, but it's incredibly rare to hear a hit record that has only a lead vocal on it. Invariably, there are other singing parts too. You don't have to add backing vocals to your arrangements, but good backing vocals will really lift them out of the ordinary.

There are three basic ways of using backing vocals in an arrangement:

- Backing vocals can be used in a similar role to instruments such as organs or strings, singing wordless 'las' or 'ooohs'.
- The backing vocals can sing some of the same words as the lead vocal to the same rhythm, but at a different pitch, creating a *vocal harmony*.
- The backing vocals can provide contrast to the lead vocal, creating a question-and-answer or call-and-response effect, or just commenting on the main lyric.

We saw that lead vocals are sometimes 'double tracked': backing vocals are almost always double, triple, quadruple or even more densely tracked, so as to sound like a group of people singing. Assuming you don't actually have access to a group of people to sing your backing vocals, it's possible to get good results by doing them all yourself, as long as you have the patience.

Occasionally you hear songs where there is a harmony vocal all the way through, but normally you would use backing vocals just where you want additional emphasis or power. In most cases this means the chorus, but don't overlook the possibility of underlining individual lines within another section of the song by adding backing vocals there, too.

If you have a lead vocal tune worked out and you know the chord sequence that fits under it, it's usually possible to come up with a good-sounding harmony line more or less by trial and error. At the point where you want the harmony to come in, work out what note the lead vocal is singing and think about what that note would sound like if you moved it up or down by an interval such as a third, fourth or fifth (up a third or down a sixth are probably the most commonly used harmonies). Pick one that sounds all right against the same chord, and you should find that if you start on that note, it's possible to sing something with almost the same 'shape' as the lead vocal line, but lower or higher in pitch.

Recording vocal harmonies takes a bit of practice. You'll probably want to finish the lead vocal first so that you have something to work to, and you need to make sure that the way you sing the harmonies parallels the lead vocal as closely as possible: if you pile up several vocals where all the words are slightly out of alignment, it'll sound messy. It can be hard to hold the right pitch for the harmony when you're used to singing the lead. If that's the case, you could try recording the harmony line on a keyboard as a guide. Remember that you can use comping, and all the other recording tricks described above, on backing vocals just as you can on lead vocals. And if it sounds good, by all means get carried away and try recording two or more different harmony lines.

The finishing touches

All of the above might sound like a lot of work, and in truth, it is: you should probably expect to spend at least a couple of days getting an arrangement together for your song, and it can take much longer. But don't be put off. It is difficult and sometimes frustrating, but it's not mindless drudgery, like taking the bins out or flipping hamburgers. By working on your arrangements, you're exercising your imagination and acquiring new skills, and the sense of satisfaction to be had from hearing your ideas grow into a finished recording is hard to beat. And, of course, the more you do it, the better you'll get at doing it.

So far in this chapter, we've looked at the different elements that go into a typical pop or rock arrangement individually. As we've seen, it's important to bear in mind at every stage how these elements will work together, especially when it comes to choosing loops, or sounds from a keyboard or software synthesizer. Once you've got the individual elements sounding right, the final stage is to think in more detail about how they should be blended so as to create a coherent whole. This is a process that's often called 'mixing', and it can encompass a number of different actions.

Probably the most important of these is getting the relative loudness of each of the elements right, or creating a 'balance'. If you're using a hardware multitrack recorder, you'll have sliders called 'faders' which you can push and pull to raise or lower the volume of individual sounds within the arrangement. In a software recording programme, the same applies, except that the faders only exist on the computer screen and have to be moved with the mouse. Either way, the principles are the same. With some of the tracks in your arrangement, you'll find you can move the fader to a suitable position and leave it there: this usually applies to bass and drums. With other tracks, particularly instruments you've recorded using a microphone, you'll find that you want to adjust the fader positions as the song plays through, to compensate for changes in loudness in the recorded track. When you do so, your recording equipment will offer you the ability to remember these fader movements, so that you can do them once and then have them replayed every time you play back your song. Look up 'automation' in the manual for more on this.

There's no foolproof recipe for creating a successful balance, but the most common mistake is to have the vocals at too low a level. The singing is the most important part of the arrangement, and it needs to be loud. Even if you feel awkward about listening to your own voice, don't be tempted to bury it by making it too quiet: a weak voice will just sound weaker if you do that. In modern rock and pop records, the drums are usually pretty loud, too. The level of the bass is often hard to get right, especially if you're listening on headphones or cheap loudspeakers.

A related concept is the idea of *panning*. Chances are the music you're making will be played back on a stereo system, with left and right speakers, and panning allows you to move the different elements of your arrangement from one to the other. Again, there are no hard-and-fast rules but in general, bass sounds (bass guitar and bass drum) should go to the centre, as should the lead vocals and, often, the snare drum. Supporting elements of the arrangement can be spread out a bit. For instance, if you have an electric guitar and an acoustic guitar, you could pan one to the left and the other to the right. Likewise, if you have double-tracked any of the instruments or voices, you can make them sound 'big' by panning one of the tracks left and the other right.

We've already looked at compression and reverb as tools for making vocals sound better, and these are useful for other tracks, too, though you wouldn't usually apply reverb to bass instruments. The normal way to use a reverb is via something called an 'auxiliary' or 'aux send'. This lets you apply one reverb sound to as many of the elements of your mix as you want, and is a great way of making them all feel as though they are happening in the same (fake!) room. One thing to be aware of is that keyboards and synthesizers tend to include their own reverb generators, so unless you've turned these off, you are likely to find that the sounds you choose already have reverb applied.

By contrast with reverbs, compressors are 'insert processors', which means that every track you want to compress has to have its own separate compressor, usually with different settings. You'll probably find that instruments you've recorded yourself are more likely to benefit from compression than the sounds coming from your keyboard or synthesizer. Note that moving the faders and using a compressor are, in effect, different ways of achieving the same thing, and it's often more precise and natural-sounding to do the former.

You'll find that your recording equipment includes a whole lot more effects and processors apart from compressors and reverbs, too. The most common are as follows:

- Equalizers or EQs: always used as insert processors, these allow you to change the *timbre* of an instrument. As with reverb and compression, it's easy to overdo things with EQ. The most common uses include adding brightness and sparkle to vocals or acoustic guitars, adding 'thump' to basses and bass drums, and making instruments sound less 'muddy'.
- Filters: similar to EQs, but more extreme.
- Delays: use as either an insert or an auxiliary processor. A delay simply repeats whatever you put into it, either once or many times depending on settings. They're often used as an alternative to reverb, but you can also create cool effects by choosing the delay time to fit the speed of your song.
- Flangers, choruses, tremolos and phasers: used as insert processors, these create a variety of 'swirly', 'trembly' or 'whooshy' effects that can add movement and interest to things like guitars and pianos.
- Distortion and 'lo-fi' effects: used as insert processors, these turn nice sounds nasty! Try them on drums, guitars, keyboards and even vocals.

Even after you've applied the finishing touches to your arrangement, you won't be able to send it out into the world unless you can transfer it to a format that everyone else can play. This usually involves 'bouncing' or 'rendering' the output from your recording equipment to a stereo file, which you can then burn onto a CD or convert to an MP3 file. Again, the manual for your software or hardware will explain how to do this. You might have the option to make MP3s directly from your recording software, but it's usually better to use the WAV format and convert it to MP3 later if you need to. One thing you need to be careful about is getting the overall volume right. Too low, and your recording will sound feeble by comparison with bought CDs; too high, and it'll be distorted and unpleasant-sounding. Your recording hardware or software will have a 'master' fader that allows you to adjust the overall volume of the output.

Listen to tracks 16 and 17 on the CD.

Creating a good-sounding arrangement and recording of your song is one way to bring it to the attention of other people. In the next chapter, we'll be looking at the other time-honoured way of getting your music out there: performing live.

playing live and forming a band

In this chapter you will learn:

- **how to get bookings to play live**
- **how to prepare for a gig**
- **how to be a better performer on stage**
- **what to do when things go wrong**
- **how to put a band together to play your songs.**

Some people write songs purely for the satisfaction of writing songs, but most of us become songwriters because there's something we want to communicate to other people. This means we have to find ways to get other people to hear our songs. One way is to record them and sell, or give away, the results. We've already looked at how to turn a raw song into a more polished recording, and in Chapter 10 we'll look at ways to get your recordings to the wider public. Before that, though, let's consider the other way to get your songs heard: playing them live in front of an audience.

There are songwriters who never learn to enjoy performing (and everyone gets nervous before a gig), but the rewards can be huge. The buzz you get from having real people listen to and applaud your music is simply impossible to beat. However, before you can enjoy that buzz, you need to get yourself booked to play some gigs. And when you get the bookings, you need to do as much preparation as possible to make sure they go well.

Where can I play?

Most towns have at least one venue that is dedicated to live music. Typically, this sort of venue will have gigs on six or seven nights of the week, they'll host touring bands as well as local acts, and most nights they will charge people to get in to hear the music. A dedicated music venue will have its own PA system, microphones and other equipment, and will usually have a resident sound engineer. Some of these venues are privately run, while others are owned and managed by local councils. Bookings may be handled in-house, but frequently, music venues delegate their booking to one or more freelance 'promoters'. Promoters often specialize in a particular style of music, so it's a good idea to find out as much as possible about which promoters put on which gigs in your area. If you play country and western, there's no point in approaching someone who runs a monthly industrial techno night. Almost all music venues have websites, and these almost always contain information about who to send demos to, and how to send them.

A lot of live music happens in other places, too. There are lots of pubs that have music on Friday or Saturday nights only, and other spaces such as cafés and churches sometimes have licences for live music. Occasional venues usually won't have their own PA or other equipment: they'll rely on the musicians to bring their own. Some of these venues have regular promoters, but more often you will need to negotiate directly with the owner or manager. Some will pay bands to play, reckoning on taking the money back over the bar; others will expect you to pay a hire fee for the space, which you can try to claw back by charging admission. Pubs that have music once a week sometimes limit themselves to 'covers bands' playing Rolling Stones songs and the like, and if they do put on original music, they'll prefer something mainstream that isn't going to scare off the casual punters.

If you're happy to perform your songs on your own, you'll find that there are almost certainly gigs in your area where you can just turn up and play, without previously having to convince anyone that you are any good! Look in the listings for 'open mic' evenings. If you have a local folk club, they'll probably have regular singers' nights, where anyone can turn up and play, but do check in advance that original material is permitted: some folk clubs are very hardline about sticking to traditional music. At an open mic or singers' night, you'll probably get to perform two or three of your songs, the audience will be friendly and supportive, and however badly you cock things up, there will undoubtedly be someone playing on the same night who's worse than you. It's an ideal way to dip a toe in the waters of live performance, and although the experience of sitting through 20-odd other singer-songwriters of variable quality can get old fast, it's also a great way to meet other songwriters and musicians who are starting out. If the promoter or folk club that's putting on the open mic night thinks you have potential, they may well offer you a 'proper' gig on another night, and if not, you can always come back and try again next time.

To get any other sort of a gig, you'll need to have a demo recording, and if you followed the advice of the previous chapter, hopefully you should have something that showcases your songs as they deserve to be heard. If not, you should think about going to a local recording studio and making a demo. The boom in affordable home-recording equipment has knocked the bottom out of the recording studio business, and as a result, it's possible to get very good deals on studio time. Either way, be honest with yourself and don't settle for a demo that doesn't do your songs justice. It doesn't need to have elaborate orchestral arrangements, and indeed, for the purpose of getting local gigs, a recording of you and your guitar will often be perfectly adequate; but make sure that it sounds good and that you're happy with the performance you gave in front of the microphone. Remember that most venues get tens or even hundreds of demos every week, so you need to present your music in as good a light as possible.

At heart, there are two things that will make a promoter want to book you. One is if they think you're going to be good; the other is if they think you're going to bring lots of people through the door. They'll be able to make up their own minds on the first point. Don't mislead them on the second. If you're confident of getting 30 people to pay a fiver to hear you, great, but don't make any promises you can't keep. A good promoter will know how to put together a show that combines established and popular acts with new singer-songwriters. A good promoter will also be sympathetic to people who are just starting out, as long as those people are honest about their situation.

These days, many promoters find it convenient to organize everything over email and the Internet, so you should make sure that your demo is available to download from a website, MySpace page or similar. We'll be looking in more detail at how to set one up in Chapter 10. Never, ever, ever send your demo as an attachment with an email unless someone specifically asks you to: send a link to your website instead.

Other promoters will expect to hear a CD. It doesn't need to be slickly presented or look like a record, but it does need to have your contact details clearly printed, both on the sleeve *and on the CD itself*. This last point cannot be over-emphasized. In a venue where 100s of demos arrive every month, sleeves and CDs often get parted and not reunited. Don't get self-indulgent and send in an entire album's worth of demos: busy promoters won't have time to listen to it. Be ruthless about picking your two best songs and no more.

The email or letter you send to present your demo should be short, friendly, to the point, and clearly tailored to its intended recipient. Above all, it needs to be realistic. Don't fill it with grandiose claims about how you're the best thing since the Beatles. Just explain who you are, give a brief description of your music and say what you're hoping to achieve by sending the demo. Many people find that coming up with an adequate description of their own music is difficult and strangely embarrassing, but it's vital information for promoters, because they need to know how to fit you into their programme. Don't fall into the trap of saying 'my music cannot be pigeon-holed' or that it's impossible to describe: doing so is pretentious, almost certainly untrue, and no help to anyone. Far better to list a couple of well-known artists who are similar in style to you. If

figure 9.1 always put your contact details on the CD itself, as well as the packaging

you've done any high-profile gigs in the past, or there's anything else that might help to sell you to the promoter, by all means mention it, but keep it snappy and don't over-hype yourself.

A sample letter or email to a promoter

Dear Mark [*Show that you bothered to find out the promoter's name!*] I'm a local singer-songwriter called Sam Inglis, and I'm sending you my demo because I'd love to come and play at the Rose and Crown. My music has been described as 'a cross between Neil Young and Scott Walker', with an intimate acoustic feel that sometimes grows into a more epic sound. I've been doing gigs in the area for about a year now, and so far, it's been going well. I've been really pleased with the response that I'm getting from local audiences, and I'm beginning to attract a bit of a following. [*This is code for 'people will come to your pub to hear me play'*] The two songs on my demo CD are taken from my first EP, 'Changing The Water', which has been out since the end of last month and has alread sold over 100 copies at gigs. Last month I supported Bobby and the Cowpokes at their sold-out tour gig at the Dog and Duck.

I've been to lots of gigs at the Rose and Crown and I think it's a fantastic venue, so I was hoping you might be able to find a place for me on one of your acoustic nights, or a support slot with a suitable touring act. If you'd like to hear more of my music, take a look at my MySpace page at www.myspace.com/teachyourselfsongwriting. Thanks for taking the time to listen to my CD, and I hope to talk soon.

All the best,

Sam

When you've sent out your demos, the first thing you can expect to hear is a deafening silence. There are a few promoters who have the time and the kindness to contact everyone who sends them a demo without prompting, but not many. You probably stand more chance of a response if you're getting in touch by email than if you've sent in a CD with your phone number on, but either way, the chances are you will have to chase them up. Be patient. If you're on the phone the day after you've sent in your CD, you'll come across as over-keen and a nuisance. A polite phone call after a couple of weeks to say 'I was wondering if you've had the chance to listen to my demo yet' is a better bet. If they haven't listened to it by then, they might even feel a pang of guilt.

Starting your own gig

If you're having difficulty getting gigs, or if you feel there's a gap in the market in your area, you always have the option of becoming a promoter yourself. This is a medium-to-large-sized commitment, which may cost you money and will certainly take up plenty of your time, but also offers plenty of potential rewards. For one thing, it means you can give yourself as many gigs as you like. For another, it's a brilliant way of getting to know other musicians and songwriters. And if your efforts as a promoter are successful enough, you might even be able to begin booking touring acts and get a name for yourself in the wider world of music.

Many music venues are actually available to anyone who's willing to pay a hire fee. This can range from a few tens of pounds to several hundred for a typical pub-sized venue, and the rate will often depend on what night of the week you book. A little negotiation will often bring the price down quite a lot, so it's worth talking to the owners about your plans. If they think you have a good idea and that you'll bring lots of people in on a quiet night, they might even let you have the place for nothing; but if you do have to pay, the fee should be realistic enough that you can recoup it by charging a reasonable entry fee, as long as you get a decent crowd. At a dedicated music venue, the hire fee should include use of the PA system, but might not include an engineer to run it. If not, you'll need to find one and pay or cajole him or her.

If you hire a space that's not a dedicated music venue, you'll need to budget for hiring a PA as well as finding an engineer, unless you're lucky enough to know someone who will lend you the equipment. Local music shops will be able to point you in the right direction on both counts, but be aware that moving PA equipment around is a colossal pain in the neck.

Publicizing your gigs

Playing a gig to an empty room is a depressing experience, and one that inevitably leads to recriminations. The promoter blames the musicians for not bringing anyone to see them; the musicians blame the promoter for failing to publicize the gig properly. It's tempting to get self-righteous and think 'My job is to play and sing: it's the promoter's job to get people through the door', but if you take that attitude, your career is likely to be a short one. Like it or not, at the majority of the gigs you play, the onus will be on you to bring in a crowd, or at least part of a crowd.

As a result, it's important to do as much as you can to help publicize gigs that you're playing, and when you play a gig that goes well, it's crucial to exploit that success for the future. If you're lucky enough to send 100 people home at the end of the night thinking that you're the best thing since sliced bread, you need to do everything in your power to make those people come back to see you again, and to buy your CDs and T-shirts. However much they love you, they can only come to your gigs if they know about them, so one essential tool for up-and-coming bands or singer-songwriters is a mailing list. Take a clipboard, some pens and some paper to every gig. If possible, pass it around the audience after you've played, or failing that, leave it at the door for people to sign up as they leave (though this is much less effective). All you need get from them is a name and an email address.

figure 9.2 if you can collect your fans' contact details, you'll be able to tell them about future gigs and CD launches

Once you have a mailing list, don't spam your fans and risk alienating them by sending out messages every few days. If you're lucky enough to have lots of gigs in a short space of time, just send one or two mails listing all of them, or focus on the one that's most important to you. And, above all, learn how to put the email addresses in the 'BCC' field of the message. Many people have strong feelings about keeping their contact details private, and no-one wants to read a mail that starts with a huge list of addresses.

There are lots of other avenues for generating publicity, including Internet message boards, local press and radio, putting up posters, handing out flyers and busking. Some of these, especially press, posters and flyers, might be dealt with by the promoter, but you should always check whether there's anything you can do to help. Local newspapers and listings magazines are the most important tools when you're publicizing a gig. It's well worth getting to know the journalists who cover live music in your area, because even a short preview in the local *Evening News* will reach tens of thousands of people, and can make the difference between a full house and an empty room. By contrast, a mention on local radio might feel impressive, but it won't have much effect. The Internet can be a useful promotional tool, but you need to be careful to target your messages at people who will genuinely be interested. Indiscriminate spamming of message boards will just get you a bad reputation.

Assuming the promoter who's booked you is any good, he or she will probably have their own ideas as to how to publicize the show, and to that end, may need some publicity materials from you. These will include a good-quality photo of yourself that you can send via email, and a 'biog'. The photo will need to be taken at a high enough resolution to be usable for print purposes, which means several inches across at 300 DPI (dots per inch); if the JPEG file is at least a few hundred kilobytes in size, it should be OK.

A biog is basically a slightly expanded version of the description you sent the promoter along with your demo, and the same points apply. Above all, your biog needs to be useful to the people the promoter will be sending it to. Those people will most likely be local journalists, and the ideal is to give them a pithy and informative paragraph or two explaining who you are, what your music sounds like, what you've achieved with it so far and what you hope to achieve in the future. If there's anything surprising or particularly unusual about your own history, so much the better; it doesn't have to relate to your music.

Preparing for a gig

So, the big day approaches. Your opportunity is nigh, and you want to make the most of it. What can you do to make sure it goes as well as possible? The first thing is to be realistic about your expectations, and what you hope to achieve. Enjoy the anticipation, but don't build the gig up in your mind to the point where it becomes a matter of life or death.

A more mundane but crucial aspect of preparing for a gig is to make sure that you have all the necessary information from the promoter. This information includes answers to all of these questions:

- What time will you be on stage?
- Who else is playing?
- How long is your set?
- What time are you expected to arrive at the venue?

- Will you get a sound check?
- How do you get to the venue, and if you're driving, is there anywhere to park?
- Do they need any publicity materials from you?
- What do they expect you to do to help promote the gig?

When you know how long your set is supposed to be, you can get to work putting together a set list. This, as the name suggests, is basically a list of songs in the order you plan to play them. Don't leave it until the night, or worse still, go on stage without a set list at all. It might sound odd, but in the heat of the moment it's easy to completely forget what songs you know and get into a blind panic. At the same time, though, keep in mind that your set list is not set in stone. If the audience is clearly reacting better to fast, bouncy songs than to quiet folky numbers, think about adjusting your performance to suit. And if, as inevitably happens, your stage time gets shrunk, decide in advance which songs to jettison.

Once you've done a few gigs, you'll quickly realize that some of your songs work better on stage than others, and you'll probably be surprised to find that your own favourites aren't always the ones that strike a chord with audiences. It doesn't take long to start thinking of some songs as your 'bankers': reliable crowd-pleasers that give you your best chance of winning the crowd over at the start of the show, or leaving them on a high at the end. Others will turn out to be less reliable, and you may well find that some never work at all, however hard you try.

Putting together a good set list thus becomes a lot easier when you have some experience to go with your intuitions, but there are a few guidelines that are worth bearing in mind:

- The most important songs are the first and the last in the set.
- Try not to put several songs back to back that are in the same key, or have the same lyrical themes.
- If you have lots of long, slow-paced songs, try to break them up with one or two more up-tempo numbers.
- Think about including a cover version that the audience might know, especially if you can think of an interesting way to rework it so that it's different from the original.
- If there are some songs in your set that you find particularly challenging to play, give yourself a break by separating them with easier ones. For instance, a song where the guitar accompaniment is all barre chords can leave your left hand in dire need of a rest!

- Make notes on the set list to remind yourself about anything that needs to be said during the performance, such as telling the audience about your CD when you play the first track from it.
- Likewise, make sure you note any technical changes that you need to make before or after a song, such as putting your guitar into a different tuning, or switching on a particular effect pedal.
- Don't assume that you're going to get an encore, but do think about what you're going to play if you do. It's perfectly acceptable to repeat something you played earlier in the set as an encore, so don't waste your best songs by reserving them for a curtain call that might not happen.

On the night

Especially if you're travelling a long way to get to a gig, it's vital to make sure you bring everything you're going to need. This includes:

- Your guitar or keyboard, plus any other instrument such as a harmonica, that is part of your performance.
- Any related equipment, such as leads, power adaptors, tuners and effects pedals, your keyboard's sustain pedal, capos, plectrums, your amplifier if you're using it, and a keyboard stand if you need one.
- For guitarists, a spare set of strings, and if you're playing an acoustic guitar, a spare bridge pin and a spare battery for the pickup.
- Your set list.
- Directions on how to get to the venue, and a phone number to call in case you get lost or held up.
- Your mailing list and some pens or pencils.
- Any CDs or other merchandise you plan to sell.

When you get to the gig, make yourself known to the promoter and the sound engineer. If it's a 'proper' gig as opposed to an open mic night, you should get the chance to do a sound check. This is an opportunity for the engineer to ensure that you will sound as good as possible to the audience, and for you to make sure that you're comfortable with what you hear on stage. It's very definitely not the time to decide to tune your guitar, or practise that song you can't quite remember.

SET LIST

Awkward — "This song's about..."
Desperation
The Story Of My Life
Air Crash Investigation
Cherchez La Femme
Rocking Horse Shit — Capo 3rd fret
For The High Jump
They Did Something
The Scheme Of Things
Little Imperfections
The Birds
I Can See The Sea — TALK ABOUT CD
Older Women
The Hardest Word — Drop D!

MAILING LIST

figure 9.3 some performers find it helpful to make notes on their set list reminding them to change tunings, put their capo in the correct position or make stage announcements

Most PA systems have two different sets of loudspeakers. The 'front of house' speakers are for the audience, while the 'monitors' or 'wedges' are for the performers on stage, and the balance of sound in the monitors doesn't have to be the same as what the audience hears. You will have to trust the sound engineer to get things right from the audience's perspective, but the sound check is a chance for you to work with him or her to get a sound in the monitors that you find comfortable. Some singer-songwriters prefer to hear lots of their own voice on stage; others like almost none. Don't be afraid to tell the engineer what you want.

Things can change between sound check and the gig proper, and if you suddenly find in mid-set that you can't hear things properly, try to catch the engineer's eye. There's a more or less universal language of gestures that you can use to communicate what's wrong. Point first to the instrument or microphone that you're not happy with, then point up in the air if you want more of it in the monitors, or down towards the ground if you want less. Or, of course, you could just bite the bullet and tell the engineer what you'd like changed.

Recording a gig

When you're playing a gig, you don't get the audience's perspective, so recording your gigs can be a great help in becoming a better live performer. You're sure to pick up on lots of details that passed you by in the heat of the moment, and think of ways to make your set and your songs more effective.

At some venues, the sound engineer will be happy to record the gig for you, as long as you supply a suitable cassette, blank CD or Minidisc. You'll need to find out in advance whether this is possible and which one of these media you should bring. The sound engineer will usually just record what is going over the PA system, and the results might sound a bit strange because the audience will be barely audible. The alternative is to record the gig yourself, by using a Walkman or other portable recorder. Sit it somewhere in the audience where you know it won't get knocked. The sound quality will be rougher, but you'll be hearing exactly what the audience were hearing. Either way, you're unlikely to get a recording slick enough to play to other people, but it'll certainly give you an honest view of your own performance.

One thing that you can expect to enjoy at every gig you ever do is plenty of hanging around, especially if you're not the headline act. The way it usually works is that the headline act (the band or artist who are playing last on the night) gets to sound check first, and because they're the most important, they often take ages to do so. After that, everyone else sound checks in reverse order, so if you're opening the show, you'll be the last to sound check, and if you're unlucky, there may not even be time for you to sound check at all. In that case you just have to walk on stage, plug your instrument in and hope for the best!

With nerves fluttering inside you, it's easy to use that time hanging around getting drunk. That will have obvious and potentially disastrous consequences, especially if you haven't had a chance to eat: don't assume that because Shane MacGowan can put on a blinding performance after two pints of sherry, that you will too.

Once you've sound checked, there's relatively little you can do to prepare further. If possible, leave your set list on stage before the gig starts, so you don't have to bring it on with you or risk forgetting it. If you have vocal warm-up exercises, you could try to find a suitable space to do them where you won't be heard. Make sure you tune your guitar just before going on stage, even if you already tuned it before the sound check: the heat from stage lights and a crowded venue can play havoc with tuning, especially if you've fitted new strings, and it looks very unprofessional if you walk on stage and then suddenly realise you need to tune up. Likewise, it's embarrassing if you stride purposefully on stage and then spend five minutes trying to remember where to plug your instrument in, or which lead to use. Make a mental note before you go on.

Oh, and if there are other people playing on the same bill as you, do them the favour of being a good audience member, even if you don't think much of their music. You'd be annoyed if they stood at the back of the room talking loudly through your set, so don't do it to them.

Dealing with nerves

Everyone gets nervous before a gig. That includes the other people you're appearing with at the Rose and Crown, and the global superstars about to walk out on the main stage at Glastonbury. The reasons why not everyone *looks* nervous are twofold. First, there's a fine line between nervousness and excitement, and the most compelling live performers are those who are able to channel their nervous energy into a fired-up stage persona. That is perhaps not something that can be taught, but some of the other aspects of a confident performance certainly can. These are skills that are sometimes called stagecraft, and the most basic ones are not difficult to learn.

The audience will only know that you're nervous if you give off signals that say you are, and it's very possible to train yourself to suppress these signals:

Microphone technique

Inexperienced singers often unintentionally sabotage their own performance by not appreciating the best way to use a microphone on stage. The most common mistake is to sing every song with your mouth jammed right up against the mic, and it's easy to find yourself doing this if you can't hear your vocals properly in the monitors. In that situation, though, it's much better to ask the engineer to make the vocals louder than to try to force the level up by getting too close to the mic. Most people sound far better if they can maintain a minimum of a couple of inches between their mouth and the microphone.

It's also crucial to remember that the human voice is a very dynamic instrument, which can cover a wide range between very loud and very quiet. This means that if you simply stand in one place, and the sound engineer doesn't adjust the level of the microphone, the loud bits will be deafening, or the quiet bits won't be audible. The solution is to use what's called 'microphone technique'. This involves moving closer to the microphone when singing quietly, and further away when you're really belting it out. Depending on your voice and the size of the venue, that could mean six inches or a foot or more. Ask the engineer in your sound check if you're uncertain.

- You'll seem nervous if you don't look at the audience, or if your eyes are constantly jumping around the room. Address your songs to specific people in the crowd, and force yourself to maintain eye contact with them if you can.
- In most venues with proper stage lighting, you'll find that you can't actually see people in the crowd, but it's still important to look at them!
- Fidgeting, shuffling from foot to foot and other small movements are dead giveaways that you're nervous. Train yourself either to stand still, or make exaggerated, confident movements. When you're not playing your instrument, clasp your hands behind your back rather than make lots of fiddly gestures that might betray nerves.
- Never bring lyric sheets or any other memory aids on to the stage, except for a set list. If you know the lyric sheet is there, you *will* forget the words; and if you need a lyric sheet to help you remember a song, you haven't learnt that song well enough to play it on stage.

- Try not to mutter or gabble anything that you say between songs.
- If you make a mistake in a song, keep going as if nothing has happened. Remember, the audience doesn't know how the song is supposed to go, so if you played the wrong chords or accidentally started with the second verse, they'll only realize if you draw attention to it.

Most important of all is to be yourself on stage, or at least to have a stage persona you're comfortable with. You sometimes come across songwriters or bands who act as though they're on stage at Wembley Arena even when they're actually playing to ten people in Daventry. A few of them have the charisma to get away with it, but most of us would be better advised to play to the audience that's actually there, not the one in our heads. If you're playing at the Rose and Crown, don't embarrass yourself by launching into any 'Hello London! Do you wanna *rawk*?' routines.

Unless you have some clever way of running all your songs into one half-hour medley, you will have to talk to the audience at some point. Many people find this to be the most difficult aspect of performing, and it's amazing how often you see singer-songwriters who can pour their heart out in their music, but are unable to even say 'Hello' to the crowd without shrivelling into a ball of nerves. If you fear that you might be one of them, for God's sake work out what you're going to say in advance. It doesn't have to be much: a few simple lines to introduce any songs that might need it, a 'Thanks very much, my name is X' at the end, and perhaps a plug for your CD or a mention of your mailing list. It's no more cheating to practise these parts of your performance than it is to practise your songs.

If things go wrong

However much you prepare for a gig, there will always be things outside your control that can upset your performance. If this happens, the most important thing is to remain calm. Most audiences are there because they want you to play well: if they can see that something has gone wrong, they'll be sympathetic, and will have the patience to wait a minute or two while you sort it out.

Here are the most common problems you can run into, and some suggestions as to what to do about them:

- **Problem:** your guitar has gone wildly out of tune.
  Solution: unless you're right at the end of your set, it's better to take a minute or two to tune it up properly than to soldier on, even if that means having to drop a song from your set.
- **Problem:** you've broken a string on your guitar.
  Solution: changing a string on stage is a last resort unless you're very experienced, because it takes a long time and the new string will very likely go out of tune in the first song. Unless you're the only musician who's playing that night, there will almost certainly be someone else in the room who has a guitar with him or her, so the best approach is to simply ask, from the stage, if you can borrow it.
- **Problem:** your instrument suddenly refuses to make any sound through the PA system, or begins to be horribly distorted.
  Solution: first, check that you haven't accidentally left your tuner pedal switched on, or knocked your instrument's volume control, or pulled out the lead, or unplugged your keyboard from the mains. Having eliminated these possibilities, it can be worth using a different cable to connect your guitar or keyboard to the PA, because cables can break too. After that, you're once again faced with the need to borrow an instrument from someone else. In the last resort, you can ask the sound engineer to set up a microphone for your guitar, if the pickup stops working, but there's not much you can do with a dead keyboard. Nine times out of ten, when acoustic guitars become buzzy and distorted it's because the battery in the pickup is running out, but it's not usually feasible to change it on stage.
- **Problem:** your microphone stand collapses, or the PA system dies.
  Solution: this is something the engineer really needs to sort out for you. A collapsing mic stand can be played for laughs, though.
- **Problem:** someone in the audience decides to heckle you.
  Solution: the options very much depend on the situation. If the heckler is one drunken and obnoxious idiot in an audience that's otherwise loving your performance, you can simply ignore him or her; if you can think of a witty put-down, so much the better. If the heckler is part of a rowdy crowd, you might find that it's impossible to stop yourself being sucked in

to a wider slanging match. If you really want to avoid that, launch immediately into your loudest and fastest song and hope to overwhelm them.

- **Problem**: people in the audience are talking during your set.
  Solution: if everyone is talking, it's a sign that you've lost the audience's attention, and you need to do something to get it back. When this happens, you'll instinctively find yourself playing and singing louder and louder in a bid to make them notice you again, but this is unlikely to help; they'll just raise their voices to compensate. Whatever you do, don't turn into a schoolteacher and start telling them off for not paying attention, or plead with them for silence. They're adults, they've paid their money on the door and they have the right to talk if they want to. The only solution is to make them not want to. Unfortunately, there's no foolproof way of doing this, but there are things that are worth trying. One is to grab their attention by doing something surprising: for instance, if you play a loud song that stops unexpectedly, you'll give them that embarrassing feeling of talking loudly over music that isn't there any more. Another is to pinpoint the most persistent or loudest talkers in the crowd and pointedly address your next song directly at them, or try to engage them in conversation between songs. Finally, a high-risk strategy that can be amazingly effective in the right hands is to unplug your guitar, jump off the stage and walk into the audience to play your next song. The idea is that this dramatic gesture will shut them up, and because you'll then be playing completely acoustically, they'll have to stay quiet to hear you.

After the gig

When you're happy with your performance and feel that you got a good reception from the crowd, don't waste that goodwill. Find a good moment to take your mailing list round and get people to sign up; often, you can simply hand it to the nearest audience member and ask them to pass it on when they're done. If possible, make sure any CDs or flyers you have are prominently displayed so that people won't be able to miss them as they leave the gig. You may be able to ask the person taking money on the door to sell CDs for you. Try not to put people on the spot by demanding to know what they thought of your performance, though. If they liked it, they'll tell you without prompting.

Sod's Law dictates that if you do a blindingly good gig, the promoter won't be there to see it, but even if he or she is, don't be too pushy in your attempts to get a repeat booking. At the end of a hard night's work, it's unlikely that the promoter will be in the mood to think about future dates in any case: a better option is a polite email or phone call the next day thanking them for the gig and asking if there's any chance of another.

Starting a band

So far, we've looked at the options that are available if you're willing to play as a solo artist with just your guitar or keyboard for support. However, most of the singers and songwriters that we hear on records and see at gigs don't perform like that. They have a band to back them. The right band can make an immeasurable difference to how well your music comes across on stage and, potentially, will enable you to make good recordings without you having to create the entire arrangement yourself. More than that, playing your own songs with a band can be a fantastic experience in its own right, even if you never leave the rehearsal room. There's something incredibly satisfying about hearing a rhythm section kick in and feeling your song transformed. Even the simple fact that other musicians actually want to get involved and play songs that you've written can be pretty gratifying in its own right.

It's a good job that being in a band can be so rewarding, because it can also be an almighty headache. There are plenty of practical hurdles to overcome, including finding times and places to rehearse and transporting people and equipment. There are also 'management issues' arising from the inevitable tensions that emerge within any tight-knit group of people. If you're the chief songwriter in the band, it's likely that you will be the one who has to deal with both the organizational hassle and the emotional baggage. And that's assuming that you can find anyone who wants to be in your band in the first place!

Putting together a band can be difficult, especially if you don't already know the music scene in your town well, but it's never impossible. Nearly all music shops will let you put up a 'musicians wanted' ad for free, and there are bound to be Internet message boards you can try, as well as the ads in your local paper. Find out where bands in your area rehearse, and put adverts up there, too. To maximize your chances of success, bear the following in mind:

- Have a clear idea in your mind of what you want the band to sound like, and what your ideal line-up would be, but don't be inflexible. For instance, if you run into a brilliant pianist who's keen to play your music, it's got to be worth a try, even if your original plan was to start a two-guitar, no-keyboard band.
- Make clear in your ad what style of music you want to play.
- Like promoters, musicians will be much more inclined to work with you if you can play them a good demo of your music. This has the added advantage that they can take the demo away and learn the songs.
- If you feel shy about asking people who are better musicians than you to join your band, remember that there are lots of great musicians out there who have never written a song in their lives. Often, they will be just as impressed by your talent as you are by theirs.
- The most difficult musicians to find are usually singers and drummers.
- If one person joins you, he or she may well have friends who they could persuade to do so.
- Even if you are having trouble finding one or two members of your band, it's often useful and worthwhile to start rehearsing with an incomplete line-up.

WANTED

Singer/songwriter seeks musicians to form a band – I'm looking for a drummer, bass player and keyboards/backing vocals, but other instruments considered! Influences: the Kinks, Blur, Kate Bush, Björk, Beach Boys...

Call Sam on 09876 543210 or myspace.com/teachyourselfsongwriting

If your band doesn't have a drummer, you may find it's possible to rehearse in someone's living room; as long as no-one plays their instrument too loudly, you'll be able to sing over the top without a PA system to amplify you. However, once you add a drum kit to the mix, you will definitely need a PA system to rehearse. Not only your singing, but also acoustic guitars and keyboards will need to be amplified to compete with a live drummer in volume.

There will almost certainly be practice facilities available for hire in your area, and it may be possible to persuade a local venue to let you rehearse on a Sunday afternoon or another time when they're closed to the public. The cost and the quality of the equipment available will vary, but hiring a rehearsal room should be easily affordable between four or five band members. Some rehearsal rooms offer the hire of drum kits and guitar amplifiers as well as a PA system, and this can be a boon if you're stuck for transport.

When you get to the rehearsal, it's important to use that time constructively. You don't need to be a James Brown-style dictator, but nor do you want to fritter away the hours on pointless jams or amusing reggae cover versions. Again, if you're the chief songwriter and singer, it will probably be you that has to offer some sort of direction to the band during rehearsal.

Getting gigs with a band is a little harder than it is for a solo singer-songwriter. If your band is a simple and quiet acoustic duo or trio, you might still be able to play at open mic nights and singers' nights, but for anything more complex, and certainly anything involving a drum kit, you'll need to convince someone to give you a 'proper' gig. Again, this is unlikely to happen unless you can give promoters a demo. You have two options: to record a demo with the whole band, or cheat and give them a demo with MIDI instruments that you recorded yourself, as we discussed in the previous chapter.

Recording with a band can be very rewarding, and there's no doubt that sooner or later you'll want to have a recording of your band playing. However, it takes a good deal of skill, lots of equipment and a suitable space to make this possible, and in most cases that means it's not practical to do it yourself. Instead, you'll need to go to a studio and hire or persuade an engineer to make a demo recording for you. The studio business is extremely competitive these days, but even so, you can expect to pay several hundred pounds to record a two- or three-song demo to a good level of quality. If that's beyond your means, one alternative is to look for colleges and universities in your area that offer courses in

Music Technology. All students on such courses have to do recording projects as part of their coursework, which means there may be someone there who'll be only too glad to record your band for nothing. However, the results you get through this avenue are likely to be patchy.

Even if you do have the money to hire a good studio, you'll make a better recording if you wait until the band has a few gigs under its belt, because all bands take time to gel. The Catch 22, of course, is that you need a demo recording in order to get those gigs in the first place. It might be cheating to give out a CD that was entirely concocted in your bedroom using software synthesizers and loops, but as long as it sounds similar to the band, it may well be the best option.

Whatever you do, though, wait until the band is really well rehearsed and 'tight' before you play your first gig. You only get to play one first gig: it's a rare opportunity to get your friends and the local music scene excited about the potential of your band, so make the most of it.

At the end of the day, playing live isn't for everyone; but whether you're strictly a bedroom musician or a seasoned performer, one means of promoting your music that you can't afford to ignore is the Internet. The right approach to web design and networking can win you more friends than any number of gigs in your home town, and in the next chapter, we'll be explaining how you can turn sites such as MySpace to your advantage.

promoting your music on the Internet

In this chapter you will learn:

- **how to set up a website of your own**
- **how to make your music available for download on the Internet**
- **how to sell music on the Internet**
- **what you can do to get people listening to you online**
- **how to use MySpace and other social networking sites to your advantage.**

Recently, the press has been full of stories about artists who signed million-pound record deals or went straight to number one purely on the strength of their online activities. Legend has it that the Arctic Monkeys, Sandi Thom and Lily Allen all rose to fame because of a grassroots Internet following that forced the rest of the world to take notice. Look a little closer, though, and most of these stories don't sound quite so romantic. For example, Sandi Thom's campaign of 'online gigging', with live shows streamed from her London basement, was certainly effective: but it was also a cleverly managed publicity stunt, masterminded by a PR agency and involving heavyweight technical support that wouldn't be available to just anyone. Likewise, although Lily Allen became a 'MySpace phenomenon', she was already signed to a major record label and working with leading songwriters and producers, so her chances of success were a lot higher than most.

figure 10.1 Lily Allen: MySpace phenomenon or marketing triumph? © Chris Floyd

What this tells us is that the Internet is a powerful tool for promoting music, but like any other tool, it needs to be operated by skilled hands. It is possible to build up a fanbase using social networking sites such as MySpace, or by filming a brilliant home video and posting it on YouTube, or by working to raise your profile on discussion forums and message boards; but it isn't easy. You need to be good at using those tools, and of course, you need to have an exceptionally good product in the first place.

Setting up a website

At the time of writing, MySpace has been so successful that lots of bands don't bother having a website of their own, relying on their MySpace page to do the same work for free. And there's something to be said for this option, because MySpace is now so popular that many music fans look first for a band's MySpace page and only later for a .com or .co.uk site. Nevertheless, there are still good reasons why you might want to set up your own site:

- If you have your own site, you can offer facilities such as discussion forums which aren't available as part of a MySpace page, and you have complete freedom over its look and feel.
- Some songwriters and musicians worry that by posting their music on MySpace they are signing away too many of their rights.
- You have no control over what happens to MySpace in the future, should the company be sold, go bust or make a decision that affects your MySpace page.
- Even if you have only a very basic website, owning the domain name, such as yourname.com or yourname.co.uk, stops anyone else from using it and protects it for the future.
- Owning your domain name will enable you to receive emails addressed to that domain, for instance at info@yourband.com.

In order to set up a website, you'll need two things: a web host and a domain name. If you have broadband Internet at home, your service will almost certainly include web hosting, and if not, there are millions of companies that will arrange it for you. By default, Internet service providers will give you a not-very-memorable subdomain such as www.yourname.yourserviceprovider.com, and it's definitely worth shelling out the small fee to buy a proper .com, .co.uk or .org address. This is easy to do online, and once you've bought yourbandname.com or whatever, you can just set it up to be routed to the subdomain your service provider has given you.

If you're reasonably good with computers, it's not particularly difficult to create a simple website by 'hand coding' HTML using a text editor, such as the *Notepad* application that comes with Windows. There are lots of HTML tutorials on the web that will hold your hand through the process and explain how to mimic all those neat effects you've seen on other websites. You can also download HTML templates and code for more complicated constructions such as online forums.

The less confident might want to use an application like Microsoft *Word*, which can export documents as HTML sites ready to upload to a website. Once you get into more complex territory, you'll probably need to either hire the services of a professional web designer or get to grips with specialist applications such as *DreamWeaver*. Whatever approach you take, make sure you test the results in as many different web browsers as possible. Most web designers spend most of their time sorting out issues with sites that look fine in *Internet Explorer* but go all funny when viewed in *Firefox*, or vice versa. Once you've created and tested your site, you can upload it to your web host using a piece of software called an FTP client. These are widely available as free downloads for both Windows and Mac OS.

Whether you go for a simple, no-frills design or an elaborate site strewn with animations and Flash movies, you'll want people to come back to your site again and again. That means updating the site with new text and pictures on a regular basis: and that, in turn, means that the design of the site needs to make it easy and convenient for you to update it. A part of the attraction of MySpace Music pages is that they make it simple to add new dates to your gig calendar and new diary entries to your blog. If the design of your own site makes you jump through hoops to achieve the same things, you'll end up neglecting it.

Putting music on your website is very easy. All you need to do is convert your recording to a suitable format – which, in 99.9 per cent of cases, means MP3 – upload it to your web host's server and put an HTML link to that file in the code for your site. Be careful about the file name: most web servers are 'case sensitive', so you need to get the capitalization right in the link, and spaces in file names can cause problems.

Making MP3 files

Most of the music-making software we looked at in Chapter 08 works with sound in Wave format, where files end in a '.WAV' extension. However, this isn't used for music on the web, because Wave files tend to be very large, making them slow to download. Instead, music is usually made available for download in 'data compressed' formats. MP3 is the most popular of these, but there are many others, including Ogg Vorbis, Microsoft's WMA format and the AAC format used by Apple's iTunes Music Store. The principle behind all these formats is the same: they reduce the size of a sound file by throwing away information that they think won't be audible to the human ear. The more information they throw away, the smaller the files get, but the more obvious the effect on sound quality.

To get your music on the Internet, you'll need to convert it to MP3 format. Many recording packages will do this for you, or you could use an application like *iTunes*, which is free to download from the Apple website. Some MP3 converters do a much better job than others, so if you're not happy with the results, it's worth trying another program. Any decent MP3 converter should give you a whole list of options, the most important of which is the *bit rate*. This is the key factor in the trade-off between sound quality and file size. It's measured in kilobits per second (kbps), and 128 kbps is the minimum setting that's likely to produce acceptable quality. With the rise of broadband, file sizes and download times are no longer such a big deal as they once were, so it pays to go for a higher setting than this, such as 192 or 256 kbps.

Setting up a MySpace Music page

Whether or not you also have a conventional website, it's definitely worth setting up your own MySpace page: it's free, and as we've already seen, is often the first port of call for people who want to find out more about you. If you type www.myspace.com into your Internet browser, you'll see a Member Login section lurking between the adverts on the right-hand side of the screen, with a big button saying 'Sign Up!'. This is the wrong place to start, because signing up here will just create a standard MySpace profile, which doesn't allow you to upload music or run a gig calendar. Instead, you need to click on the Music entry in the list that runs horizontally near the top of

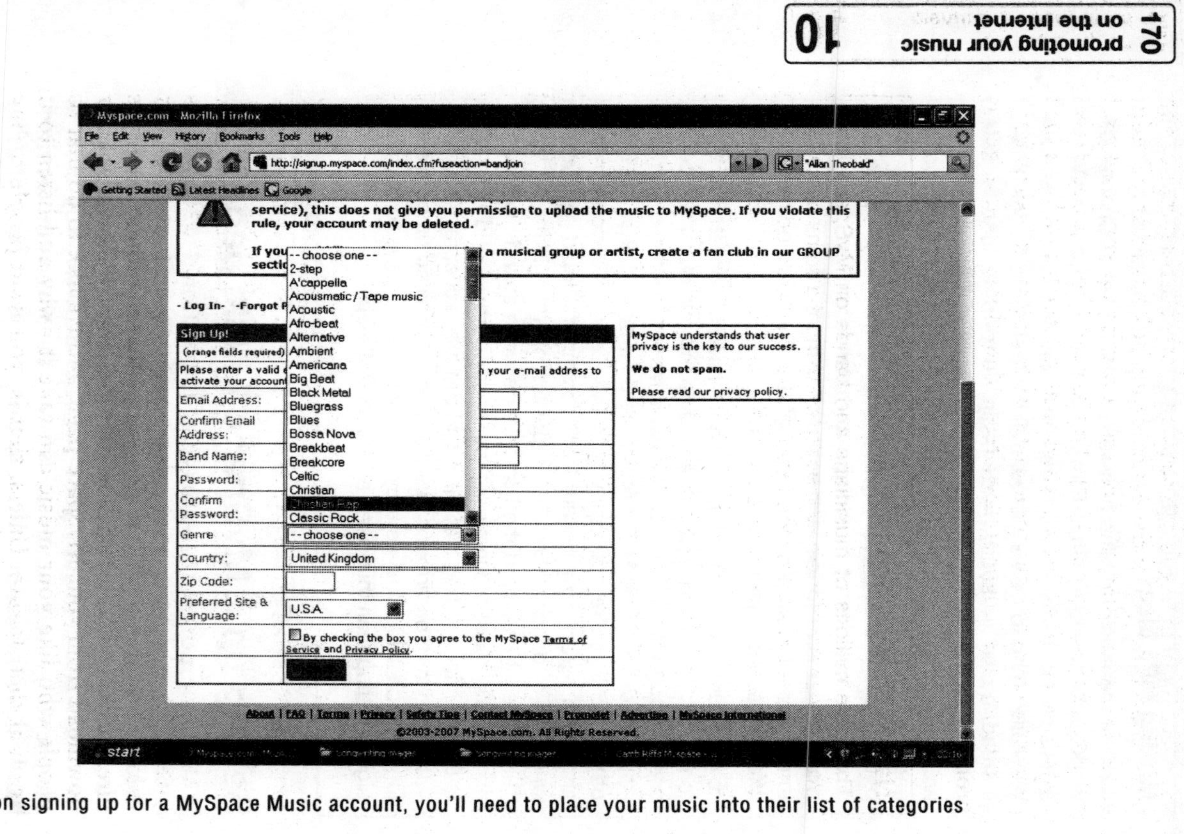

Figure 10.2 on signing up for a MySpace Music account, you'll need to place your music into their list of categories

the page. From here you can search for other artists' music, and more importantly, click the Artist Signup link buried at the right-hand side. After that, the process of setting up your MySpace page is pretty self-explanatory. You have to choose three genres in which your music belongs, and although the list includes such recherche styles as Emotronic and Christian Rap, it doesn't have a category for singer-songwriters. The closest you'll get is probably Acoustic.

Names on MySpace

There are millions of musicians and bands on MySpace, and inevitably, many of them turn out to be using the same names as some of the others. However, you're at a significant advantage if you're the first person or band with your name on MySpace, because that way, you lay claim to the myspace.com/yourname URL, so people won't have to use MySpace's irritating and unreliable search tool to find you. For example, there are numerous bands with MySpace pages who call themselves Resistance, The Resistance, Resistance Is Futile and so on; doing a MySpace Music Search for 'Resistance' brings up almost 90 bands, but completely fails to find one of the most prominent of the bands with this name (Cambridge's The Resistance, at www.myspace.com/thepsychedelicresistance). If you do find your name already taken, you might want to think about choosing a more distinctive one for your musical activities, with the hope of avoiding this fate.

Your MySpace page can be used to host up to four of your songs. One of these will start to play as soon as anyone visits the page, and you have the option to play the same track for every visitor, or choose one at random. The music you hear automatically when you click on someone's MySpace page is 'streamed', which means you don't have to wait to download it before you listen to it, but also means that the sound quality is dire. However, it's also possible to make your MP3s available for download from your MySpace page, and it's nice to do that so people who like your music can take it away and listen to it again at their leisure. Unless, that is, you want people to buy your music rather than download it for free, in which case you can still use the streamed version as a 'taster', but link to the shop or website where your music is available for sale (we'll consider how to do this in a minute).

MySpace hacks

One of the features that has made MySpace popular is the way you can customise it. By default, everyone's MySpace page looks the same, but with a little ingenuity, it's possible to make quite radical alterations to their appearance. If you hide the adverts, though, you risk getting your profile deleted. You can even add extra features to your page such as tour maps, speech, video chat, games and literally hundreds of others. Do a Google search for 'MySpace hacks' and you'll find more than you could possibly want, or there's an official beginner's guide at www.myspace.com/profilesupport.

Unfortunately, the popularity of MySpace has also made it an attractive target for malicious hackers, and you need to be on your guard to avoid having your profile hijacked. To trick users, hackers create links to fake MySpace login pages which they can use to harvest your login details. Avoid clicking on any suspicious links, and if you're asked to enter your login details, always check that the URL displayed in your web browser begins with 'http://login.myspace.com'.

As well as music, MySpace pages can host photos and blogs, and include a gig calendar that's very easy to use. They also offer two ways to communicate with other MySpace users: comments, which are displayed on the recipient's page for all to see, and messages, which are private. The idea that made MySpace a hit, though, is Friends. Making 'Friends' on MySpace is a lot easier than it is in real life: you visit someone's profile and click on 'Add to Friends'. Next time they log on, they'll be asked if they want to approve your request. If they do – and if they have no reason not to, they usually will – you'll appear in their list of Friends and they in yours.

The idea behind the Friends system is a brilliant one, because it eggs everyone on to be madly competitive about gathering more and more Friends. There are people on MySpace with tens of thousands of Friends, and if you have the time and the inclination, it wouldn't be difficult to join them. Friend requests are very rarely refused, so there's nothing to stop you spending evening after evening sat at your computer, clicking on MySpace pages almost at random; and if you do so, you'll soon build up a list that looks impressively long. You can even get semi-automated computer programs that will find and add Friends to your profile.

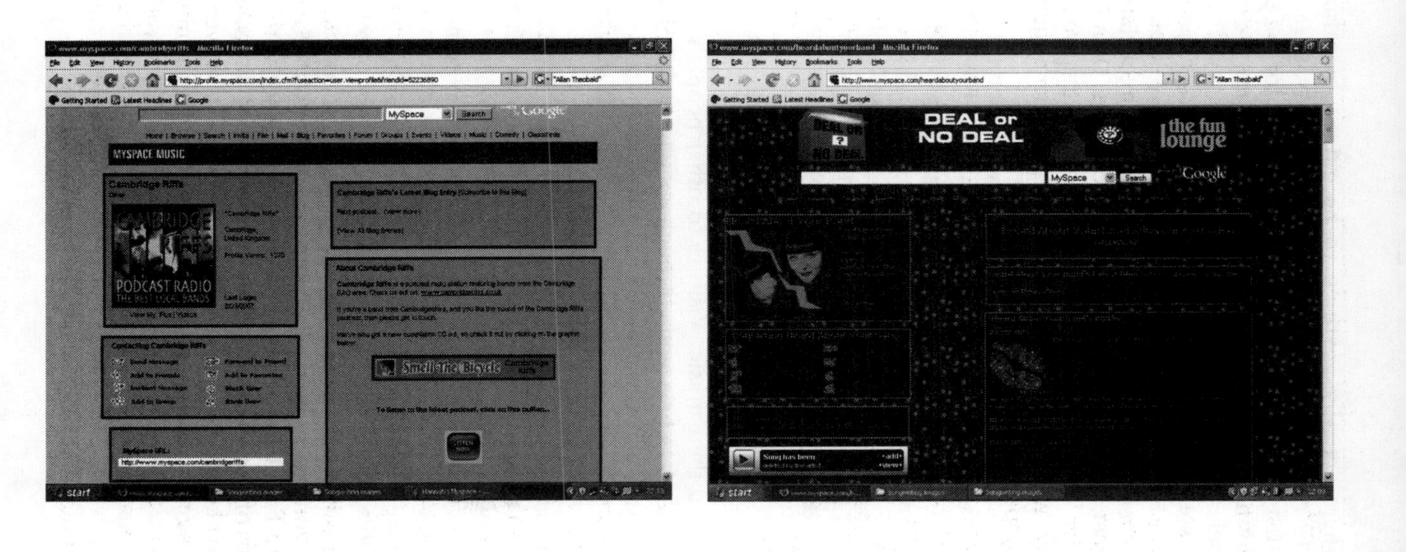

Figure 10.3 it's possible to make radical changes to the way your MySpace profile looks

But is there actually anything to be gained by taking this approach? Amassing 8,000 randomly chosen MySpace Friends might satisfy the collector's instinct in you, but for the purpose of promoting your music, you're better off making the effort to find people who might actually like your music, and trying to build up some sort of relationship with them. You also need to set up your own MySpace page so as to make it as easy as possible for people to find you, if they're looking for the style of music you make.

- Your profile includes lists of influences and other acts you sound like. It's worth putting a good number of names in each, because people often look for new music by searching on the names of bands they already know and like.
- Lots of established artists have MySpace pages of their own. You're unlikely to strike up a personal relationship with them that way – if they're important enough, they probably employ someone else to look after the page in any case – but these can be a good starting point for finding other people who share your tastes.
- When you invite someone to be your Friend, it's always a good idea to leave a comment that shows you've actually listened to their music. Visitors to other people's MySpace pages will often find yours through comments that you leave.
- It also pays to look at the comments left by fans on other people's MySpace pages. If they like band X, maybe they'll like you, too.
- The Internet allows you to make friends with anyone, anywhere in the world, but from the point of view of furthering your music career, Friends who are local to you are more likely to make a practical contribution by turning up at your gigs.
- MySpace allows you to send Event Invitations to other members, and some people use this as a way of telling the world about their gigs and CD launches. However, anyone with more than half a dozen MySpace Friends receives hundreds of these invitations, and many people never even look at them, so this is emphatically not a good alternative to your email mailing list.
- You'll get a huge dose of publicity if you can persuade MySpace to make you one of their Featured Artists. Why not email them and ask?

Other websites

MySpace isn't the only game in town. There are other social networking sites, and some, like Bebo.com, can be used in a similar way to gain exposure for your music. There are also lots of online forums devoted either to music in general (such as www.drownedinsound.co.uk), or to specific genres (such as www.americana-uk.com) and artists. These are good places to find potential fans, but be very careful how you approach them, because the last thing you want to do is come across as an indiscriminate spammer. Far better to become an active member of the forum and make yourself known to other members before you try to get them interested in your music.

Some musicians have also gained a lot of exposure thanks to the video sharing site YouTube.com, the most famous example being the band OK Go. If you can think of a brilliant idea for a low-budget video, as they did, you should definitely try it out. If it takes off, your video might even get picked up by one of the satellite music TV channels.

Internet radio is another field that's worth investigating. Most FM and AM radio stations are commercial enterprises supported by advertising, which means they have to play music that people know. That, in turn, means limited opportunities for new and unsigned artists to get their music on the air, especially if their music is out of the mainstream. By contrast, Internet radio is much cheaper to produce, so there are more stations that are willing to take a punt on new music, and many that specialize in particular genres. Why not look for stations playing music that you like, and ask them to listen to yours? Thousands of Internet radio stations are hosted at www.live365.com, so that's a good place to start looking.

There are also plenty of websites designed especially for promoting new and unsigned artists. One of the most successful of these is Garageband.com, which creates an audience for new music by forcing users to listen to and review other people's songs before they can post their own. Whether this will really generate an audience for your music is debatable. Like MySpace and many other sites, Garageband.com are keen to share stories about bands who were 'discovered' on their pages and went on to sign to major record labels; but if you do want to get a conventional record contract, don't rely on the Internet alone. Hard-bitten record company executives won't be impressed by how many MySpace Friends or Garageband reviews you have, and word of mouth is still the currency that rules the music business. Making a name for yourself as a great live performer and doing a few high-profile gigs in London will have a hundred times the impact of anything you could hope to do in the online world. Whatever you do, don't get suckered into paying money to websites that promise to promote your music for you. It's unlikely to achieve anything except making you poor.

Selling your music on the Internet

It used to be the dream of every struggling singer-songwriter to sign a recording contract with a major record label, and in the 1960s and 1970s, there was really little alternative if you wanted to make records. Recording an album was a horrendously expensive business, and even if you could arrange that, getting records pressed and distributed to shops without the involvement of a big record company would have been phenomenally difficult.

Nowadays, it's perfectly possible to make and sell an album without involving anyone else at all. It's still difficult to achieve global mega-stardom without some help, but succeeding on an independent level will put you in a much better position to negotiate with record labels, publishers, managers and the other music industry types who might be able to offer that help. If you want to get your music into the shops, you'll still need to cut a deal with a distributor who's willing to put it there, but if you have a computer, you probably have all you need to start selling music on the Internet.

One thing you need to decide is whether you want to sell CDs, or downloads, or both. There's still a lot to be said for having a physical product such as a CD to sell: many music buyers are more comfortable handing over cash for something tangible, rather than an electronic download, and having a CD available also gives you a ready-made demo to hand to promoters and record companies. On the down side, making CDs costs money. You can duplicate small numbers of CDs yourself with a computer and a printer, but this is a pain in the neck. The alternative is to pay someone else to duplicate them. For quantities smaller than 300, the only realistic option is to have your CD duplicated on CD-Rs (making it, in essence, no different from the CDs you can make at home): this will cost you perhaps £150 for 100 CDs. If you're making 500 or 1,000 CDs, you can use the same duplication method as the professionals, which involves creating a 'glass master' of your disc and having CDs manufactured at a proper pressing plant. This will be less expensive in terms of cost per CD, but isn't practical for small numbers of discs. To find CD manufacturers and duplicators, do a Google search or look in the classifieds section of *Sound On Sound* magazine.

A big advantage of CDs over downloads is that you can sell them at gigs, and perhaps by mail order from your website, without needing to set yourself up to take credit card payments. However, if you want to go beyond this, there are lots of online record shops that offer online ordering using credit cards, which certainly makes the whole thing easier for customers. Obviously, though, these shops will take a percentage of the sale price. Perhaps the best-known online shop dedicated to selling CDs by unsigned artists is www.cdbaby.com; they charge a $35 setup fee for taking on your CD, plus $4 commission on every CD they sell. It's also non-exclusive, so there's nothing to stop you signing up with other online music shops as well. If you take this route, it's probably worth signing up with at least one UK-based online store, since otherwise your CDs could end up travelling across the Atlantic and back before they end up in customers' hands. Provided your CD looks and sounds reasonably professional, you shouldn't have difficulty finding online shops willing to stock it.

It's even easier to get your music onto websites that sell downloads, because your MP3 files won't be taking up valuable space in a warehouse somewhere. By far the most successful of the legal downloading sites is Apple's iTunes Music Store, and you might be surprised to learn that it's fairly easy to make your music available for sale there. What you need to do is find an iTMS 'aggregator' such as AWAL UK (www.awal.co.uk). As long as they are happy that your music is sufficiently well recorded, they'll upload it to the iTMS on your behalf and take a small commission on any sales you make; at the time of writing, about half of the 79p retail price makes its way to the artist after Apple and AWAL have taken their cuts.

Selling your music is like selling anything else, only more competitive, and you can't expect to just sign up with CD Baby or the iTunes Music Store and watch the cash roll in. You need to make potential buyers aware that you exist, and persuade them to listen to your songs, before you can hope to shift any CDs or paid-for downloads. In a crowded market, that isn't easy, but if you use them right, tools such as MySpace can definitely help.

11 the professional songwriter

In this chapter you will learn:

- **what opportunities exist to make money from your skills**
- **how to develop your career as a songwriter**
- **how to write for and with other people.**

If there's one dream that's shared by almost everyone who writes songs, it's that of getting paid to do it. Even if your day job is well-paid and rewarding, the idea of making a living from songwriting instead is bound to appeal. After all, why spend all day in an office when you could sit around at home with a guitar and a cup of coffee, bash out a hit when inspiration strikes and wait for the royalty cheques to roll in?

If that's how you imagine the life of a professional songwriter, think again. Of course, being able to write great songs is a basic requirement for making a living as a songwriter, but you need to be able to do far more than that. As with everything in the music business, networking and 'people skills' are essential if you want to make money from your songs. You need to be as comfortable in the conference room as you are in the recording studio, and most of all, you have to be able to put someone else's idea of what makes a good song above your own.

You'd expect songwriting to be a fiercely competitive business, and it is, but you might also be surprised at how diverse the opportunities for songwriters can be. The most obvious, and for many people the most creatively satisfying, outlet for a songwriter is to be the artist who records and performs your songs as well as their writer. We've looked at how you can start a career as a performer in Chapter 08, and in Chapter 09 we examined some ways to promote your recordings. In this chapter, however, we'll be concentrating on the opportunities that are available to songwriters who are unwilling or unable to try to be pop stars in their own right. There are lots of reasons why you might feel that this applies to you, whether you're simply uncomfortable with the limelight, reluctant to live out of the back of a van for a year, or concerned that you might not have a powerful enough singing voice or image.

The obvious alternative is to write songs for other people who are willing and able to become pop stars in their own right, and that's what we'll be focusing on in this chapter, but there are less travelled roads that are also worth considering:

- Library music, or 'production music' as it's sometimes known, is big business. Library music mostly consists of pastiches of commercially released music in any and every style, including mainstream pop and rock songs, but it's not created to be sold directly to the record-buying public. Instead, it's designed to be used by film, television and advertising companies in situations where they need a semi-recognisable piece of music, but can't afford the time or money to license a 'real' hit song.

- TV and radio production companies and advertising agencies also sometimes commission music directly from songwriters. For instance, programmes aimed at young children feature a lot of original songs, while radio uses a lot of 'jingles', which are in essence just short songs.
- There is a certain amount of 'corporate work' available, involving writing songs for businesses. These might consist of company anthems, or pieces of music to mark a particular event such as a large conference.
- Songwriters also have a role in the theatre, most obviously in the creation of musicals. Very few new musicals make it to the West End stage these days, but amateur theatre companies and schools still need material.
- Under some circumstances it's possible to get funding from bodies such as the Arts Council, even for projects that aren't conspiciously 'arty'. The Arts Council in your area may well have some sort of programme devoted to helping new writers and performers.

Publishing

If you're a performer and a recording artist, you get to make albums by signing a recording contract with a record label. Doing so is a fairly pivotal moment in your career: in many cases, it marks the point at which someone goes from being an amateur touring the country in a clapped-out Transit van to a professional with a large team of specialists on hand to shape their sound and their look, and to sell their music to the world. It also means you suddenly get paid quite a lot of money, although this will just be an advance against the royalties the record label expects your albums to make. It is, in other words, something that means you've 'made it' as a musician, at least up to a point.

Performers who write their own material nearly always sign another sort of contract at about the same time as their recording contract. This will be a contract with a publishing company, and just as with a recording contract, a publishing contract will give you an advance against royalties. The difference is where the royalties come from.

To understand music publishing, you need to know that there are two kinds of copyright in a music recording, and as a result, there are two basic ways that recordings of your music can generate money for you. Copyright exists both in the song, and in the recording of that song, and the two copyrights often don't belong to the same owner.

Copyright in a recording is indicated by a symbol that looks like a P in a circle. Most record contracts will stipulate that the copyright in the recording is owned by the record label, and that some percentage of the income generated by that copyright will be passed on to the artist. So, if you are the artist, you'll get paid a percentage on every copy of your recording that sells. You'll get additional income when your recording is played on the radio or TV, and you'll even get some money when that record is played in public, such as on a jukebox in the pub, or by a DJ at a nightclub.

Copyright in the song itself is separate, and is indicated by the more familiar C in a circle. The owner of the copyright also gets paid in all the above situations, regardless of whether they recorded the song, or whether someone else did. This can be a source of friction in bands where there is one main songwriter, because the recording royalties will have to be split between four or five band members, while the songwriting royalties – which can be as much or more – will just go to one.

The recordings made by its artists are a record company's main assets, and the record company makes its money by exploiting those assets: selling CDs and downloads, licensing recordings to film and television soundtracks, and so on. It's up to them to sell as many copies of their recording as they can, collect the money and distribute a share to the artist. Publishing companies, likewise, exist to exploit the copyright in songs, although they don't usually own that copyright. Instead, the songwriter signs an agreement with the publishing company, whereby the publisher agrees to exploit the writer's material in return for a percentage of whatever revenue it generates. Again, publishers will usually offer an advance when a deal is signed.

Lots of wannabe songwriters focus their efforts on getting a contract with a music publisher, because they think about publishing contracts in the same way that aspiring performers think of recording contracts: once I get one of those, I'll have 'made it'. However, there are a number of reasons why this approach is flawed.

First, publishing contracts are not like recording contracts. Performers need to get into bed with record labels, because the labels have the power to help them make albums, get them into the shops and get them noticed. The same is not true of music publishers; there's no sense in which you need to sign a publishing contract before you can make records. Copyright exists automatically in any song you write (in the UK and Europe), and in theory, it should be possible for you to collect any money that your songs make without having to go through a publisher. That's not to say that publishing companies have no use: if you're lucky enough to get into a situation where your songs are being recorded and making money, you may well find that you need the help of a publisher to keep track of everything, but even so, the longer you put off signing a deal, the better deal you'll be able to strike.

From the publisher's perspective, there's no point in signing a contract with a writer unless they're confident that that writer is going to make money. However good your songs are, they won't make any money unless people record them. Many newcomers assume that signing a publishing contract will solve this problem for them, because it's the publisher's job to 'place' songs with artists. That's true, but only true up to a point. Music publishers have a duty to do their best to exploit whatever songs are in their catalogue, but it's not the only focus of their business, and the idea of signing a songwriter who is wholly dependent on their efforts to place songs is not going to appeal. That's why it's attractive to sign publishing deals with artists who record their own material: the publisher knows that the songs are going to be recorded and released, so they can expect to generate enough income from the copyright to pay off the advance and make a profit. Similarly, a publisher will be happy to sign a contract with a songwriter who's already enjoying hits, because they know that they can start taking their 15 or 20 per cent straight away; many writers get songs placed through their own contacts, or by a manager, rather than by their publisher. By contrast, handing out an advance to an unknown songwriter who doesn't record his or her own material is a long shot. To do it, a publisher will need to be utterly convinced that your material has commercial potential, and in return for taking that risk, they'll expect a larger cut than they would with an established songwriter.

Getting your songs in the public eye

If you want to pursue a career as a professional songwriter, you're unlikely to get very far if all you do is send out demos to every publishing company in the country. So what's the alternative?

It's crucial to remember that songwriters don't only work with artists and publishers, and there are lots of people in the music industry who have the power to help you out, if only you can convince them that you're good. Managers, press officers, recording engineers, record producers, session musicians, radio programmers, video directors, journalists and record company employees of all stripes all have the potential to be useful, while lawyers who specialize in the music business now wield a lot of influence.

Something else to bear in mind is that no matter who you're dealing with, sending them an unsolicited demo is the least effective way of persuading them that you're brilliant. People in the music industry will take you and your music much more seriously if you're introduced personally by a contact they know. Anyone who receives lots of demos will be very used to hearing lots of bad demos, and will probably regard listening to them as a chore rather than a pleasure, so if all they know about you is that you've sent them a CD out of the blue, they'll expect your music to be bad. If, on the other hand, you can engineer a situation where they actually want to hear your music, perhaps because someone they trust has told them how good it is, they're infinitely more likely to like it.

But how do you engineer that sort of situation if you're not involved in the music business and have no contacts? The answer is that you need to cultivate those contacts, and although that's something you can't expect to do overnight, it's certainly possible. One good starting point would be to join the Performing Rights Society and the Mechanical Copyright Protection Society. You'll need to do this in any case if you have any success, because it's these organizations that collect royalties on your behalf. However, they also run lots of events aimed at career development, where you'll get the chance to meet and learn from people in the music business. These provide excellent opportunities for networking. Other organizations are well worth investigating, too, including the British Academy of Songwriters and Composers and the Music Producers Guild.

For every aspiring songwriter like you, there are also lots of people around who aspire to do all the other music-business jobs we just listed, and some of these people will go on to be influential in the business. So why not get to know them before they acquire the coke habit and the company Bentley? Get involved in your local music scene, figure out who is going places and make friends with them. Does your local community or student radio station have one show that stands out as being slicker and more professional than the rest? Find out who the producer and presenters are and introduce yourself. Look at the local fanzines and What's On magazines, and get to know the music editors. And above all, make yourself known to as many local musicians and managers as you can. Getting in 'on the ground floor' with a promising singer will put you in the perfect position to kick off your career as a songwriter if he or she has any success.

Personal relationships and word of mouth are always crucial in the music industry, so you should never ignore opportunities in your area, where you'll have the chance to co-write in the traditional way, working in the same room as your partner. Equally, though, the Internet has opened up great opportunities to work with people on the other side of the world. Networking tools such as MySpace are perfect for meeting the up-and-coming artists and music business types you'll need to know, and broadband makes it easy to send ideas and finished tracks to people wherever they are.

Copyright

A lot of songwriters get slightly paranoid about the idea that someone else might rip off their material and claim it as his or her own. The music industry is full of dubious business practices, but this particular problem happens to unknown songwriters very, very rarely, and most of them worry about it far too much.

Let's face it, the reaction of your average record company executive on being confronted with a pile of hundreds of demos to listen to is not going to be 'Great, I bet there's something in here I can steal!' More likely is that they'll be thinking unprintable thoughts about the torture of having to sit through hundreds of awful demos. And in the unlikely event that one of the demos strikes that executive as being brilliant, he or she stands to gain far more by forming a lasting partnership with the songwriter who sent it in, than by illegally claiming it as their own. The challenge for new songwriters is not stopping other people from stealing your work: it's getting them to listen to your work in the first place.

In fact, it's arguable that paranoia about being ripped off, combined with an increasingly litigious approach to business, has done far more harm then good for songwriters. Many record companies in the United States now refuse to even listen to unsolicited demos, and will return them unopened; as far as they're concerned, it's better to risk missing out on something brilliant than to open themselves up to lawsuits from unknown songwriters who claim that the new Britney Spears hit resembles the demo they sent in four years ago. If you want to get these record companies to listen to your songs, you'll need to convince a well known music-business lawyer to stop by and play them on your behalf. It all means more cash trousered by the legal profession and fewer opportunities for new songwriters.

That said, it's certainly worth knowing your rights, and doing your best to avoid situations where there might be a difference of opinion as to who owns the copyright to a song. As British and European law stands, copyright in your songs belongs to you, from the moment you write them, and regardless of whether they are ever recorded, published or released commercially. That is technically true in the United States, too, but practically speaking, it's difficult to enforce any copyright claim unless the copyright is registered with the Library of Congress.

No similar registration scheme exists in the UK, so many people try to create their own proof of authorship. This usually involves recording a song, placing a copy in a Jiffy bag and posting it to yourself by Special Delivery. The idea is that you can then produce the unopened, but postmarked and dated, Jiffy bag in court if you need to demonstrate that you wrote the song before a certain date. This might give you a sense of security, but it's hard to find cases where it's actually made any difference in a legal battle.

You're far more likely to get ripped off by friends and associates than you are by complete strangers, and some of the nastiest copyright disputes come about when a song that is co-written for fun by a group of people goes on to become a surprise hit. It's not always easy to sit down and discuss business in the middle of a creative brainstorming session, but it pays to get written agreement about who wrote what, and who owns what proportion of the copyright.

Writing for other people

You might be surprised to learn that many supposedly 'manufactured' pop groups or singers take a very active role in shaping their material. There's a reason why Robbie Williams has a co-writing credit on nearly all of his hits: it's because he's made a major contribution to writing them. The worst mistake you could make as a songwriter would be to assume that the person you're writing for is an idiot who knows nothing about music. If a singer cares enough about his or her craft to want to do it professionally, he'll usually have spent a lot of time thinking about what he wants to do, and what works best for his voice and image. Don't think that you know better than the artist what sort of material he or she should be recording.

The other fatal mistake you can make is to be cynical about the job. Lots of novice authors think it must be easy to bash out a Mills & Boon-style potboiler to make some fast money, but in fact, the only ones who get published are those who take it seriously and are capable of enjoying romantic fiction in an unironic way. And similarly, lots of novice songwriters hear hits like James Blunt's 'You're Beautiful' and think 'That's rubbish, anyone could write a song like that!' But if you think it's somehow beneath you to write songs like that, you'll never understand what it is about those songs that strikes a chord with the audience, and you won't be able to reproduce it.

To have any chance of success as a professional songwriter, you'll need to be able to write songs with other people, adapt to their preferred way of working, and most of all, to 'get' what it is they are trying to achieve. The best way to learn these skills is through practice, which is another good reason why you should look for up-and-coming local singers to work with, rather than trying to leap in at the deep end and write the next Sugababes hit. Most established artists have probably got used to co-writing in a particular way, but if you have the chance to work with a newer singer or group, you'll have more freedom to direct things, and in all probability, more time to work on songs.

Range finding

If you're writing for someone else, it's important to know in advance what the range of his or her voice is. In other words, find out what their highest and lowest notes are, and make sure your lead vocal part doesn't stray outside those limits. Be prepared, in any case, to have to transpose your songs, because it's not always possible to predict what will be the most comfortable key for the singer to sing them in.

Dynamite demos

Throughout the book we've emphasized that it's both possible and necessary for songwriters to be able to make good-sounding recordings of their songs, and that's especially the case if you're writing professionally. To stand any chance of getting your song released by an established artist, you need to be able to create a demo that will convince both the artist and their record company of its potential. In particular, if you're sending in a song for them to evaluate, rather than writing with the singer, it's crucial that your demo has a good enough vocal performance. If you can't deliver that yourself, find a singer who can and have him or her record the demo vocal.

The positive side of all this is that if your demo is good enough, the artist and label may decide that it doesn't need to be re-recorded, so you may find that the arrangement you laboured to create in your bedroom actually makes it onto the shelves of HMV. The final version of Kylie Minogue's massive hit 'Can't Get You Out Of My Head' was changed very little from songwriter Rob Davis's original demo; likewise, the Sugababes' first hit 'Overload' was one of the demos that got them their record deal.

'Change a word, take a third'

As a new songwriter working with an established artist, you may well find yourself pressured into giving them a co-writing credit and a slice of the songwriting royalties even if you wrote the whole song almost entirely by yourself. This is unfair, but unfortunately, it's also common practice. Elvis Presley's manager, 'Colonel' Tom Parker, was notorious for insisting that songwriters give up half the publishing royalties for any song that Presley recorded. Dolly Parton famously turned down the opportunity to have Elvis record 'I Will Always Love You' for this reason, but many others were willing to agree to those terms: after all, 50 per cent of the royalties on a song recorded by Elvis Presley is a lot more money than 100 per cent of a song recorded by no-one.

A room of one's own

If you're serious about writing with other people, you'll need to be able to offer them the right sort of environment in which to do it. You might find inspiration in a bedroom strewn with dirty linen and mouldy coffee cups, but it's unlikely to create the right impression on people you're working with. Many professional songwriters have dedicated studio rooms, either in their houses or in separate premises. It's sometimes possible to rent small studio spaces relatively cheaply, but if you can't find or can't afford one of your own, it might be worth asking around to see whether there's anything you could hire or borrow for writing sessions. Whether you're working in your own space or someone else's, though, you need to be confident and capable at operating the musical equipment you plan to use. The last thing you want to do is to undermine someone's confidence in you by spending 15 minutes looking for the On switch on an electronic keyboard, or being unable to record the session because you're not familiar with the way the studio is set up.

Every songwriting partnership works differently, but there are some possible models that you might follow:

- The songwriter writes and records the entire song and sends it to the singer, who listens and makes suggestions as to how it should be changed or improved.
- The songwriter writes an instrumental with a melody and sends it to the singer, who writes the words.
- The songwriter writes a backing track without a melody; the singer writes the words and the tune.
- The singer writes the words and gives them to the songwriter to turn into a song.
- The singer has written a great chorus, but can't think of a verse, so turns to the songwriter for help.
- The singer and songwriter meet up for a brainstorming session where they try to come up with some great hooks and catchy ideas; then the songwriter goes away and works those ideas up into finished songs.
- The singer or their record company comes up with directions as to what they want the song to sound like ('We're looking for a classic disco meets hair metal feel, but with Irish folk instrumentation...'), and perhaps a title; the songwriter tries to write something that fits this brief.

These last two are probably the most typical in the modern music business, and if you're working with anyone established, you can expect writing and production to be, on occasion, a tortuous process whereby your masterpiece gets bounced back and forth between artist, management and record company people, each of whom will have strongly held and contradictory views about what needs to be done to make it a hit.

To succeed as a professional songwriter, you'll need to be able to overcome all the obstacles outlined above, and more. It won't be easy, and however talented you are, you can't afford to be a prima donna about your songs. The customer is always right; and if that means sticking a gratuitous heavy metal section into the middle of the best ballad you've ever written, you'll just have to grin and bear it. But if you're skilful and lucky enough to make it, you'll have one of the most rewarding jobs in the world. How many of us get paid to create something that is enjoyed by millions of people every day?

index

Illustrations are shown by italics.

12-bar blues chord sequence **63–5**

Acid Pro software **34, *35*, 37, 111**
acoustic guitars ***14*, 15–18, 125–8**
active monitors **32**
'All Along the Watchtower' **76**
Allen, Lily **166**
alliteration **94**
amp modelling software **126**
amplifiers **7, 9**
'Anarchy In The UK' **79, 94**
Apple Macs **28–9**
arrangements
  advice **131–2**
  bass lines **123–5**
  drum programming **118–23**
  equipment for **111–18**
  general **110–11**
  guitars **125–8**
  keyboards **128–30**
  other instruments **130–1**
arranger keyboards **22–3**
Arts Council funding **180**
assonance **93**
audio interfaces **117**
  see also soundcards
authenticity **90**
Auto-Tune **137**
automated pitch correction **137–8**
auxiliary (aux send) **141**

backing vocals **138–40**
'Baker Street' **40**
balance **140–1**
bands, starting **161–4**
bars **52–3**
bass guitars **123, *124*, 126**
bass lines **123–5**
beats **52–3**
Bebo.com **175**
'Big Yellow Taxi' **94**
biogs **151**
'Biology' **107**
bit rates **169**
blues scale **56**
bouncing **142**
'A Boy Named Sue' **104**
brass instruments **131**
bridges **106–7**
British Academy of Songwriters and Composers **183**

capos **17, 128**
CD Baby **177**
CDs, manufacturing **176–7**
(Central Processing Units) CPUs **29–30**
chord boxes **60–1**
chord circle **64, 74–5**
chord sequences **62–4, 71–81**

chords **51, 56–9, 60–6, 68–9, 70**
choruses **104–7, 142**
clichés **96**
click tracks **119**
'Common People' **87, 94**
compression **138, 141**
computers **13, 26–37, 112–18**
condenser microphones **118, 134, 136**
consonants **45–6**
contracts **180–2**
controller keyboards **25–6, 34, 112–13, 115**
copyright **180–2, 184–5**
corporate work **180**
CPUs (Central Processing Units) **29–30**
'Crazy In Love' **110**
'Creep' **40, 76**
Cubase software **115, *116,* 120, *121***

'Dedicated Follower of Fashion' **105**
delays **142**
demo recordings **145, *146,* 187**
digital audio workstations **115**
digital guitars **13**
DIing (direct injection) **126**
distortion **142**
domain names **167–8**
'Don't Look Back In Anger' **79**
double tracking **128, 137, 139**
downloads **176–7**
drum programming **118–23**
drum tracks **52–3**

effect pedals **12, 20**
'Eleanor Rigby' **87**
electric guitars **7–13, *124,* 125–8**
electric organs **25**
electric pianos **20**
electro-acoustic guitars **16–17**
email/letter example **147–8**
equalizers (EQs) **142**

faders **140**
feminine rhymes **94**
Fender guitars **10, 11, *124***
Fender Rhodes piano **20**
file formats **142, 169**
filters **142**
'Firestarter' **39**
flangers **142**
flats **55**
folk clubs **145**
funding **180**

Garage Band software **28, 34, 37**
Garageband.com **175**
'Get Back' **97**
Gibson guitars **10, 11**
gigs
  for bands **163**
  common problems **158–60**
  and nerves **156–8**
  promoters **144, 146–8, 151**
  publicity **149–51**
  recording **155**
  sound checks **153–5**
  venues **144–9**
'Girls And Boys' **69, 124**
'Golden Brown' **79, 100**
'Groove Is In The Heart' **124**
guitar parts **70–1**
guitar tuners **18**
guitars
  acoustic ***14,* 15–18**
  bass **123, *124***
  electric **7–13**
  general **5–7**
  recording **125–8**

hackers **172**
half rhymes **94**
Hammond B3 organ **25**
harmony **51–2, 139**
'Harper Valley PTA' **104**
headphones **31–2, *33,* 118, 128**
'Heart of Glass' **100**
hecklers **159–60**

'Hey Jude' **107**
hollow bodied guitars **11**
home keyboards **22–3**
hooks
  building from **81–2**
  and chord sequences **73–81**
  and chords **68–9**
  developing **44–8**
  examples **39–40**
  production **40–1**
  and rhythm **69–73**
  vocal **42–4**
humbucking pickups **8, 11**

insert processors **141, 142**
instruments **5–6**
    see also guitars; keyboards; pianos; violins
internal rhymes **94–5**
Internet promotion
  general **166–7**
  MySpace **167, 169–74**
  selling your music **176–7**
  websites **167–8, 175–6**
Internet radio **175**
intervals **53–6, 64, 65**
inversions **61–2, 71–3**
iTunes Music Store **177**

'Jailhouse Rock' **97**
'Jeepster' **100**
jingles **180**

keyboards **5–7, 18–26, 34, 53–5, 71, 111–13, 115, 128–30**
keys **59**

laptops **29**
latency **117, 118**
'Layla' **107**
letter/email example **147–8**
library music **179**
Line 6 **13**
live performances *see* gigs
Live software **34, *35*, 37, 111**
lo-fi effects **142**
loops **34–7, 53, 70, 111, 119–20**
loudspeakers **31, 32**
lyrics
  details **101–2**
  function of **84–5**
  importance of **84**
  meaning of **97–9**
  and metaphors **99–101**
  rhymes **93–7**
  and truth **90**
  and voice **86–9**
    see also vocal hooks

mailing lists **149–50, 160**
major chords **56–9**
major scales **56–9**
'Make Me Smile' **40**
Mechanical Copyright Protection Society **183**
melody **51–2, 58–9**
metaphors **99–101**
metonyms **101–2**
meter **91–3**
    see also stressed syllables
microphone technique **157**
microphones **117–18, 134, 136**
middle eights **107**
MIDI (Musical Instrument Digital Interface) **25–6, 34, 112–13, 115, 120**
minor chords **56–9**
minor scales **56–9**
mixing **140–1**
MP3 converters **169**
MP3 files **142, 169**
multi-core CPUs **30**
Music Producers Guild **183**
music theory **50–1**
music venues **144–9**
Musical Instrument Digital Interface (MIDI) *see* MIDI
MySpace **167, 169–74**

Nashville Numbers system **65**
'The Needle and the Damage Done' **102**
nerves (before performing) **156–8**

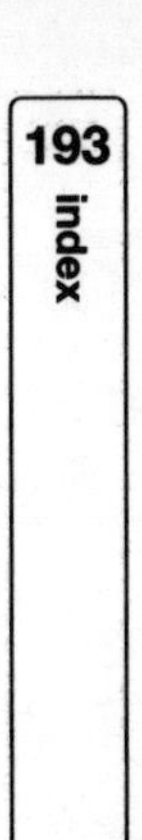

'Blue Monday' **40**
newspapers **150**
noise pollution **31**
notation **59–60**
notes **51, 53–5**
nylon-strung guitars **15**

octaves **53–5**
online forums **175**
online music shops **177**
open mic evenings **145**
opening lines **42**
organs **25**

PA systems **149, 154–5**
'Pablo Picasso' **62**
panning **141**
partnerships **188–9**
'Peaches' **124**
pedal notes **73**
percussion instruments **119**
perfect rhymes **93**
Performing Rights Society **183**
personification **100**
phantom power **117**
phasers **142**
photos **151**
pianos **18–22**
pickups **11, 16–17, 126**
playing live *see* gigs
the Pod **13**
pop shields **137**
powered monitors **32**
pre-digital synthesizers **25**
'Pretty Woman' **69**
Pro Tools software **115, *116*, 117**
production hooks **40–1**
production music **179**
promoters **144–9, 151**
publicity **149–51, 182–4**
publishing **180–2**
publishing contracts **180–2**
punk **76**

quantizing **122**

radio, Internet **175**
RAM **30**
range finding **186**
reading music **59–63**
recording
  with a band **163–4**
  guitars **125–8**
  and songwriting **26–7**
  vocals **132–40**
recording machines **134, *135***
rehearsals **163**
rendering **142**
reverberation **138, 141**
Rhodes piano **20**
rhyme schemes **96–7**
rhymes **91, 93–7**
rhyming dictionaries **37**
rhythm **51–2, 69–73, 91–3, 118–19**
rhythm guitars **127, 128**
rhythm section **123–4**
root notes **58**
royalties **180, 187**

sample letter/email, to promoters **147–8**
sampling **36, 40–1**
scales **56–9**
selling, online **176–7**
semitones **56**
sequencers **115**
set lists **152–3, *154***
setting up (guitars) **12**
sharps **55**
'She's Leaving Home' **87**
similes **100**
singing **132–8**
single-coil pickups ***8*, 11**
'Smells Like Teen Spirit' **40, 62**
social networking sites **175**
  see also MySpace
software **28, 34, 37, 111, 115–17, 126, 127**
software synthesizers **115, 129, 130**
song structures **104–8**

songwriting partnerships **188–9**
'SOS' **110**
sound checks **153–5**
soundcards **34, 117**
stage pianos **20–2**
stagecraft **156–8**
'Stairway to Heaven' **100**
'Stan' **132**
staves **59–60**
steel-strung guitars **15**
stressed syllables **45, 69, 94–5**
see also meter
strings **130–1**
studio rooms **188**
subjects, for lyrics **97–9**
swing beat **53**
syllables **45–6, 69, 94–5**
synthesizers **23–5, 115, 129, 130**

tablature (tab) **60**
'Tainted Love' **110**
'Take Me Out' **107**
tap tempo **69–70**
'Taxman' **124**
technology, and the music industry **3**
tempo **69–70**
tenses **89**
'Terrapin' **94**
title lines **42–3**
tones **56**
toolkit, for songwriting **3–4**
'Town Called Malice' **124**
transposing **63**
tremolos **11, 142**
'Trouble' **40**
truth, and lyrics **90**
tuners **18**
tunes, catchy **39, 41**
tuning **18, 19, 156**
twelve-bar blues chord sequence **63–5**

valve amps **9**
the Variax **13**
velocity sensitive keyboards **19**
venues **144–9**
verses **104–7**
violins **130**
virtual drummer programmes **122**
vocal comping **136**
vocal harmonies **139–40**
vocal hooks **42–8**
vocal range **46**
vocals, recording **132–40**
voices **86–9**
vowel sounds **45–6**

'Walk on the Wild Side' **40, 76**
'Waterloo' **79**
WAV files **142, 169**
websites **167–8, 175–6**
weighted action **19**
'Wild Thing' **62**
Windows PCs **28–9**
'Wonderwall' **73, 100**
workstation keyboards **111–13**
workstation synthesizers **23–5**
writing music **59–63**

'Yesterday' **92, 96, 105**
'You Get What You Give' **106**
'You're Beautiful' **39–40, 84**
YouTube.com **175**

teach
yourself®

Bridge
British Empire, The
British Monarchy from Henry VIII, The
Buddhism
Bulgarian
Business Chinese
Business French
Business Japanese
Business Plans
Business Spanish
Business Studies
Buying a Home in France
Buying a Home in Italy
Buying a Home in Portugal
Buying a Home in Spain
C++
Calculus
Calligraphy
Cantonese
Car Buying and Maintenance
Card Games
Catalan
Chess
Chi Kung
Chinese Medicine
Christianity
Classical Music
Coaching
Cold War, The
Collecting
Computing for the Over 50s
Consulting
Copywriting
Correct English
Counselling
Creative Writing
Cricket
Croatian
Crystal Healing
CVs
Czech
Danish
Decluttering
Desktop Publishing
Detox
Digital Home Movie Making
Digital Photography
Dog Training
Drawing
Dream Interpretation
Dutch
Dutch Conversation
Dutch Dictionary
Dutch Grammar
Eastern Philosophy
Electronics
English as a Foreign Language
English for International Business
English Grammar
English Grammar as a Foreign Language
English Vocabulary
Entrepreneurship
Estonian
Ethics
Excel 2003
Feng Shui
Film Making
Film Studies
Finance for Non-Financial Managers
Finnish
First World War, The
Fitness
Flash 8
Flash MX
Flexible Working
Flirting
Flower Arranging
Franchising
French
French Conversation
French Dictionary
French Grammar
French Phrasebook
French Starter Kit
French Verbs
French Vocabulary
Freud
Gaelic

Russian Grammar
Sage Line 50
Sanskrit
Screenwriting
Second World War, The
Serbian
Setting Up a Small Business
Shorthand Pitman 2000
Sikhism
Singing
Slovene
Small Business Accounting
Small Business Health Check
Songwriting
Spanish
Spanish Conversation
Spanish Dictionary
Spanish Grammar
Spanish Phrasebook
Spanish Starter Kit
Spanish Verbs
Spanish Vocabulary
Speaking On Special Occasions
Speed Reading
Stalin's Russia
Stand Up Comedy
Statistics
Stop Smoking
Sudoku
Swahili
Swahili Dictionary
Swedish
Swedish Conversation
Tagalog
Tai Chi
Tantric Sex
Tap Dancing
Teaching English as a Foreign Language
Teams & Team Working
Thai
Theatre
Time Management
Tracing Your Family History
Training
Travel Writing
Trigonometry
Turkish
Turkish Conversation
Twentieth Century USA
Typing
Ukrainian
Understanding Tax for Small Businesses
Understanding Terrorism
Urdu
Vietnamese
Visual Basic
Volcanoes
Watercolour Painting
Weight Control through Diet & Exercise
Welsh
Welsh Dictionary
Welsh Grammar
Wills & Probate
Windows XP
Wine Tasting
Winning at Job Interviews
Word 2003
World Cultures: China
World Cultures: England
World Cultures: Germany
World Cultures: Italy
World Cultures: Japan
World Cultures: Portugal
World Cultures: Russia
World Cultures: Spain
World Cultures: Wales
World Faiths
Writing Crime Fiction
Writing for Children
Writing for Magazines
Writing a Novel
Writing Poetry
Xhosa
Yiddish
Yoga
Zen
Zulu

Life Coaching
Linguistics
LINUX
Lithuanian
Magic
Mahjong
Malay
Managing Stress
Managing Your Own Career
Mandarin Chinese
Mandarin Chinese Conversation
Marketing
Marx
Massage
Mathematics
Meditation
Middle East Since 1945, The
Modern China
Modern Hebrew
Modern Persian
Mosaics
Music Theory
Mussolini's Italy
Nazi Germany
Negotiating
Nepali
New Testament Greek
NLP
Norwegian
Norwegian Conversation
Old English
One-Day French
One-Day French – the DVD
One-Day German
One-Day Greek
One-Day Italian
One-Day Portuguese
One-Day Spanish
One-Day Spanish – the DVD
Origami
Owning a Cat
Owning a Horse
Panjabi
PC Networking for Small Businesses
Personal Safety and Self Defence
Philosophy
Philosophy of Mind
Philosophy of Religion
Photography
Photoshop
PHP with MySQL
Physics
Piano
Pilates
Planning Your Wedding
Polish
Polish Conversation
Politics
Portuguese
Portuguese Conversation
Portuguese Grammar
Portuguese Phrasebook
Postmodernism
Pottery
PowerPoint 2003
PR
Project Management
Psychology
Quick Fix French Grammar
Quick Fix German Grammar
Quick Fix Italian Grammar
Quick Fix Spanish Grammar
Quick Fix: Access 2002
Quick Fix: Excel 2000
Quick Fix: Excel 2002
Quick Fix: HTML
Quick Fix: Windows XP
Quick Fix: Word
Quilting
Recruitment
Reflexology
Reiki
Relaxation
Retaining Staff
Romanian
Running Your Own Business
Russian
Russian Conversation

Gardening
Genetics
Geology
German
German Conversation
German Grammar
German Phrasebook
German Verbs
German Vocabulary
Globalization
Go
Golf
Good Study Skills
Great Sex
Greek
Greek Conversation
Greek Phrasebook
Growing Your Business
Guitar
Gulf Arabic
Hand Reflexology
Hausa
Herbal Medicine
Hieroglyphics
Hindi
Hindi Conversation
Hinduism
History of Ireland, The
Home PC Maintenance and
Networking
How to DJ
How to Run a Marathon
How to Win at Casino Games
How to Win at Horse Racing
How to Win at Online Gambling
How to Win at Poker
How to Write a Blockbuster
Human Anatomy & Physiology
Hungarian
Icelandic
Improve Your French
Improve Your German
Improve Your Italian
Improve Your Spanish
Improving Your Employability
Indian Head Massage
Indonesian
Instant French
Instant German
Instant Greek
Instant Italian
Instant Japanese
Instant Portuguese
Instant Russian
Instant Spanish
Internet, The
Irish
Irish Conversation
Irish Grammar
Islam
Italian
Italian Conversation
Italian Grammar
Italian Phrasebook
Italian Starter Kit
Italian Verbs
Italian Vocabulary
Japanese
Japanese Conversation
Java
JavaScript
Jazz
Jewellery Making
Judaism
Jung
Kama Sutra, The
Keeping Aquarium Fish
Keeping Pigs
Keeping Poultry
Keeping a Rabbit
Knitting
Korean
Latin
Latin American Spanish
Latin Dictionary
Latin Grammar
Latvian
Letter Writing Skills
Life at 50: For Men
Life at 50: For Women